The Mind and Beyond

The Mind and Beyond

CONTENTS

Where Monsters Lurk amid Heaven's Secrets

Is it a ghost they are chasing?'' asks a neuroscientist as he reflects on the continuing and frustrating quest for understanding of the human mind. "Or something concrete and measurable?" Such questions come more easily than answers: How does the physical brain relate to thought and consciousness? Does the self—an individual's mental being—reside in some secure corner of that organ? Or is each of us a mere flurry of electrochemical activity flickering across the spaces between minuscule cells, vulnerable as an unstored computer message in a thunderstorm? After centuries of increasingly scientific study, the human brain—and the mind, if that is a separate entity—remains among the most enigmatic phenomena in the cosmos.

Even theories of the brain that have wide scientific support trail clouds of mystery in their wakes. Deep within the roughly three-pound mass of pinkish gray matter, for instance, far below the more recently evolved outer surface where activities like logic and language formation are believed to occur, squats an old brain section called the cerebellum. The cerebellum coordinates the body's muscles. Some believe it is also home to terrifying ancient creature images that refuse to be

banished from human awareness—werewolves, vampires, demons—and, moreover, may be the source of paranormal experiences, such as the spirit voices that speak through entranced mediums.

Among the mind's amazing riddles are uncanny abilities sometimes linked to disabling brain disorders. Victims of a strange syndrome called synesthesia, for example, receive messages from their senses through a brain switchboard gone haywire; they may taste colors, feel flavors, and see sounds. Some can read while blindfolded, by passing their fingertips over the page. And people known as savants may have the intelligence of preschoolers yet be able to memorize an entire telephone book in a single reading. Many of them reportedly possess a capacity for extrasensory perception as well.

But the most intriguing puzzle is also the most basic—the very nature of the mind itself. Like many other philosophers of the past, sixteenth-century Italian cosmologist Giordano Bruno believed the human mind was divine and contained all the secrets of heaven. In the Western world, science eroded that view over the centuries until the very opposite was generally held true: The mind could be nothing more nor less than the sum total of the physical brain's activity. Recent decades have witnessed a profound and surprising shift in this attitude among many thinkers, some of them scientists, as the accounts that launch this exploration of the mind's marvels and mysteries will show.

CHAPTER 1

The Cosmos Within

ne day in 1973, an elderly gentleman marched up a hill behind his farm-house outside Montreal carrying a basketful of old cans of house paint. When he reached a large boulder on the slope of the hill, he took brush in hand and began painting a series of images on the surface of the rock. First he wrote *pneuma,* the Greek word for "spirit"; next he painted a torch, representing the enterprise of science; then, on the other side of the rock, he drew a human head, a brain within it, and at the brain's center, a question mark. Finally, he connected all the images with a solid line.

The man was eighty-two-year-old Wilder Penfield, an eminent Canadian neurosurgeon, then retired and writing what would prove to be his last book, *The Mystery of the Mind.* The work dealt with the relationship of mind, brain, and science, and the strange hieroglyphs he had painted on the rock expressed Penfield's conviction that in time scientific study of the brain would illuminate all the secrets of the mind.

During his long career as a skilled brain surgeon and astute observer, Penfield had added significantly to scientific understanding of how the body's most complex organ works. He had developed several neurosurgical treatments for brain injuries, particularly for epilepsy. At the end of his career, he was convinced that all the varied responses of the human mind—the feelings, desires, thoughts, dreams, and perceptions that together make up consciousness—were caused by chemical and electrical interactions among the brain's billions of tiny nerve cells. Thus the capabilities of the mind, Penfield held, were determined wholly by the physical activity within the grapefruit-size lump of pinkish gray matter encased by the skull.

Yet, a year and a half after his first painting safari—and a mere six months before he died—Penfield made another trip up the hill carrying paint bucket and brush. Swaddled in sweaters to protect against the frigid winter winds, he revised his artwork. When he had finished, the painting illustrated a very different principle from that of the original: Where there had been a solid line of confidence joining the images on both sides of the rock, there was now a broken line of uncertainty. At age eighty-four, after half a century spent shoring up the prevailing scientific position, Penfield had had a change of heart. It is highly improbable, he admitted with that dashed line, that a strictly physical approach will ever yield a full explanation of consciousness. The mind, Penfield was saying, is far more than a by-product of the material brain's ability to process information.

Penfield's apostasy graphically illustrates a major breach that has divided the multitudes of scientists, philosophers, and theologians who through the centuries have delved into the nature of the human mind. Roughly speaking, a battle line has been drawn between two camps: On one side are the so-called materialists, who believe that mental processes—thoughts, feelings, the ability to reason—are merely a result of neurons firing within the brain. On the other side are the dualists, who hold that the body is a physical entity and the mind a spiritual one; each exists separately, they believe, with little or no interaction or influence on one another.

For almost three centuries, since Isaac Newton proposed his elegant clockwork universe, the austere scientific tenets of the materialists have governed Western exploration of the brain and consciousness. Mystical and spiritual approaches to an understanding of the mind have largely been dismissed as fancies lying outside the strict boundaries of scientific inquiry. Yet that same span of time has seen a number of scholars and scientists, among them Wilder Penfield, defect from the classical camp. More and more, these learned men and women have begun to suspect that the many-splendored

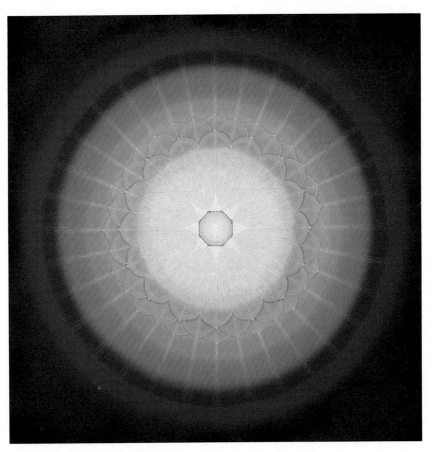

realm of consciousness cannot be explained solely by physical phenomena. As Penfield himself put it shortly before he died, "the consciousness of man, the mind, is something not to be reduced to brain mechanisms."

In the field of neuroscience, studies of human brains damaged by birth defects, accident, illness, or surgery have revealed that these afflicted people sometimes exhibit perplexing mental and perceptual capabilities that seem to some brain researchers to emanate from a "second self" or inner spirit. These observers believe they have glimpsed signs of a higher will that appears to draw its power not from the physical being but from some nonmaterial source beyond the reach of scientific instruments. In exploring altered states of consciousness induced variously by dreams, meditative trances, and drugs, they claim to have found hints of a larger, unseen spiritual reality underlying the physical world; an attunement to this invisible realm, they speculate, may account for such psychic phenomena as precognition, psychokinesis, and a sense of enlightenment or oneness with the universe.

Even more surprising, support for this shift in thinking about the mind has come from the "hardest" science of all, physics. Ephemeral puzzles about the nature of consciousness are not normal concerns for physicists, but as they have probed deeper into the strange environs of the subatomic world, these scientists have discovered that within the atom, the orderly rules of behavior governing larger objects such as baseballs and planets no longer apply. Here, matter and energy become all but indistinguishable, and the predictability of the Newtonian universe gives way to probability, to the iffiness of dice games and weather forecasting.

From the quantum perspective, the universe is not only a collection of mechanical components, like a Tinkertoy, but is also an indivisible whole, and all its parts, including the human mind, act on and are acted on by every other part. Some well-respected physicists have gone so far as to contend that without the perceiving mind of human beings, the universe as we know it would not exist at all—the mind, they say, may be the lens that focuses a world of random events into the ordered reality we perceive.

Speculations like this uncannily echo the ancient teachings of Eastern mystics, who professed the interconnectedness of consciousness and cosmos centuries before the emergence of scientific inquiry. Occasionally employing logic but more frequently relying on intuition, the founders and practitioners of such Eastern religions and philosophies as Hinduism, Buddhism, and Taoism conceived holistic portraits of the universe in which mind and matter merge and flow seamlessly one into the other. For example, more than 1,500 years before quantum physics was developed, a basic text of Buddhism called the *Avatamsaka Sutra* taught that consciousness and the material world, which to the unenlightened mind appear irrevocably divided from one another, are in fact joined in a smooth continuity known in Sanskrit as the *dharmakaya,* or "body of the great order."

As awareness of these converging world views has grown in the West, the study of consciousness, its origins and operations, has emerged as one of the most important intellectual pursuits of the late twentieth century. To many anxious observers, Western culture seems bent on a disastrous course of ecological exploitation and unbridled acquisitiveness, and some philosophers are suggesting that only a totally new approach to the understanding of consciousness—what Kenneth Pelletier, a popular author on the subject, describes as "a new science of conscious-ness"—will set society on a straighter path. Pelletier predicts that the order of thought that favors the material over the spiritual and separates the ephemeral mind from the physical brain will give way to a new, holistic order, which melds the two seemingly contradictory strains.

The debate over the origins of consciousness has been raging since at least the time of Plato. The Greek philosopher was among the first to argue that the human mind was an entity unto itself, existing independently of the body. And although anatomically he placed the mind within the brain, he denied any intercourse between the two. The brain, Plato believed, was a sphere—the perfect geometric shape, according to ancient Greeks—and thus a fitting repository for what he considered the essence of humanity.

During the Middle Ages, Christian philosophers developed their own theory about the seat of consciousness, one that perpetuated the dualistic mind-body split: God was the source of all thoughts and feelings, and these emanated from a point just a few inches above the head. Beginning about the fifteenth century, the natural sciences began to challenge the Church's view of the universe. But it was in the hands of seventeenth-century French mathematician and philosopher René Descartes that echoes of Platonic dualism, the Church's sacred order, and the prevailing logic of the day would mutate and merge to form the school of thought known as Cartesian dualism.

From the age of twenty-three, René Descartes's ambition was to develop a universal, scientific method of reasoning; one which, when applied to any type of data, would offer up conclusions that would be readily verifiable. Only when the results in every science were as certain as those achieved in mathematics, he believed, would the claim to have obtained knowledge be justified. By applying the disciplines of science, with its rigorous pursuit of empirical proof, to matters of philosophy, Descartes effectively devised the ground rules by which Western science would abide for centuries to come.

Descartes earned his commanding influence by the

Philosopher René Descartes is captured at his work in this late-1700s portrait. The Frenchman was a devout Catholic and rooted his writings on the human mind and other topics in firm convictions about the beneficence of God and the immortality of the soul. Nonetheless, Church officials banned his books in 1663, finding blasphemy in his assertion that the body was like a machine.

brilliant range and sheer volume of his scholarly output. In addition to defining the guiding principles of the emerging scientific outlook, he advanced the practice of analytic geometry, teased out the laws of mathematical physics, and explored a diverse number of philosophical issues from the essence of the soul to the nature of freedom.

Such ruminations eventually led him to divide the world's myriad aspects into two basic categories, or "simple natures": the physical, which included all physical properties and actions; and the mental, which encompassed all thoughts, feelings, and desires. Descartes discerned that human beings combined the two natures, but he decreed that the physical and mental arenas were essentially distinct—that is, neither had more than a limited effect on the other. Of the two, the philosopher considered the realm of

thought the most exalted: It belonged distinctively to humans. In fact, asserted Descartes, thought was the singular trademark of the human soul, "which needs no space to exist in, and does not depend on any material thing" for its vigor. In his scheme, the thinking mind was a gift from God and issued from the spiritual plane. Like Plato before him, Descartes lent anatomical credibility to his theory by locating the seat of the "rational soul," or mind, in the brain. He even went so far as to pinpoint a spot at the top of the brain called the pineal gland.

This tiny, tear-shaped body, which is believed to play a significant role in sexual maturation and in adaptation to changes in seasons and light, is also known as the third eye, and it was believed by some ancient cultures to have mystical powers. Descartes, though, decided that the role of

The pineal gland (above) sprouts from a part of the brain called the diencephalon. Modern scientists suspect that the organ may play a role in regulating sexual instincts, but Descartes thought it served a broader purpose in mediating between the body and the mind. In the diagram at left, he sought to show how the pineal gland might alert the nervous system to the sensation of heat.

the pineal gland was to act as a point of contact for the body and the mind. By way of the gland, he speculated, the mind propels a bloodlike fluid called animal spirits through the body to stimulate movement in the nerves and muscles. Conversely, changes in the body as perceived by the sense organs are transmitted by the same animal spirits to the pineal gland; there the fluids deliver their sensory messages to the mind. What a person perceives, then, according to Descartes, is not the sight of an actual chair or the breeze-ruffled curtains at an open window but instead the flow of the spirits within the brain produced by the eyes' signals.

Thus reality was only indirectly perceived. Descartes could never be sure what the reality of "chair" or "curtains" was, but he knew without doubt that he was *thinking* about them. Thought was the only thing he was sure of—hence his famous dictum, "I think, therefore I am."

In venerating consciousness as a manifestation of God's work, Descartes's dualistic approach seemed to put further study of the mind outside the scientist's venue. God took care of mental (that is, spiritual) matters; a scientist's proper concern was confined to physical things that could be measured, weighed, and tested. Yet it was Descartes's great insights on the logic of scientific discourse, among other factors, that led later scientists to denounce his insistence on a separation of mental and physical activity. For eighteenth-century critics of Cartesian dualism such as French physician and philosopher Julien Offroy de La Mettrie or English philosopher Thomas Hobbes, the only supportable position for a thinking person on the mind-body problem was materialistic monism—the theory that all things in nature, from waves on the shore to a person's memories or desires, were material in essence and could ultimately be unraveled with reference to physical laws.

Hobbes contended that humans were automatons, driven by the stirrings of atoms in their brains much as machines are driven by springs and wheels. La Mettrie was particularly impressed by the engineering attainments of the day—among his favorite technological achievements was a celebrated mechanical duck that could paddle and "digest" food—and he contended in a 1748 essay that the soul was merely "an enlightened machine."

Common sense seems to argue that feelings, such as anger or love, have an influence on physical behavior. But strict materialists like Hobbes and La Mettrie found it inconceivable that a subjective mood could possibly have an effect on the functioning cells of the brain. They were convinced that the insubstantial web of mental activity could be the result only of physical processes, and was not a ghostly manifestation of the divine. They began to advance a dominant materialistic argument: If science could fully map the structure of the brain and monitor the coursing of the blood and communication of the nerves, all the mind's activities would be shown to be by-products of material interactions.

In the context of the nineteenth-century Victorian Age, which was inclined to celebrate all things mechanical, materialism attained the status of dogma, and a wave of interest in the natural sciences swept through intellectual circles and popular culture alike. After Charles Darwin and Alfred Russel Wallace elucidated the theory of natural selection in 1858, natural historians strove to trace the origin of consciousness in the starkly mechanistic perspective of evolution. Scientists became obsessed with the goal of determining how, when, and why consciousness had evolved.

Certainly not all scientists embraced Darwin's theories about evolution, but those who did reasoned that the emergence of a sophisticated consciousness must have provided humans with an adaptive advantage, or else it would not have become part of our standard equipment. Like the ability to swim or to fly, the ability to think—and to be aware of the process—had to have conveyed a benefit to humans that made it more likely that the offspring of parents possessing the trait would thrive over those who lacked it. Theories abounded. Perhaps consciousness enabled human beings to work together more efficiently, so they could better carry out the tasks of feeding and defending themselves. Or maybe consciousness served to aid them in predicting the outcome of actions in an environment ever bristling with threats, thus increasing the odds of avoiding injury or death.

As these evolutionary speculations were bandied about in the period leading up to and following the turn of the century, students of consciousness were confronted by a basic question: What is consciousness, and do only humans have it? The American psychologist and philosopher William James defined consciousness as "the pursuance of future ends and the choice of means for their attainment." By this measure, James found that even a headless frog could be said to have consciousness.

Experiments conducted on a frog whose head had been surgically removed had shown that if one of the frog's legs were bound in place and electrically stimulated, another leg would reach up to bat away the source of the irritation. To James, this was clearly a purposeful gesture and indicated that, by his definition at least, the frog was conscious. Carrying out systematic observations of the animal world, other investigators detected similarly complex behaviors in a wide range of creatures from amoebas to wasps to baboons.

The notion that "lower orders" of creatures might be able to think upset Victorian sensibilities. Instead of confronting the biases of the era, some Victorian scientists deemphasized the importance of consciousness in general, even for humans. Theorists such as Shadworth Hodgson and Thomas Henry Huxley, both British, argued that mental awareness was like a decoration on a building: It added interest but served no real purpose. Hodgson used another analogy in writing about feelings, saying they were "mere colors laid on the surface of a mosaic which is held together by its stones and not by the colors." Huxley, in 1896, called human beings "conscious automata," implying that the mind had no influence on humankind's activities or evolution. Today, Princeton psychologist Julian Jaynes describes this concept as the "helpless

spectator" theory of consciousness. By this way of thinking, according to Jaynes, "consciousness can no more modify the working mechanism of the body or its behavior than can the whistle of a train modify its machinery or where it goes. Moan as it will, the tracks have long ago decided where the train will go."

Here and there, a few voices were raised from within the scientific establishment in dissent from this uncompromising materialism. One was that of Alfred Russel Wallace, codiscoverer with Darwin of the principles of natural selection and evolution. Born in 1823, Wallace worked as a schoolmaster, surveyor, and architect before developing an interest in botany. He became an ardent naturalist who undertook expeditions in the Amazon River basin and in the Malay Archipelago to collect insects. It was during such an expedition in 1858, Wallace later wrote, that, while in the throes of a fever, "There suddenly flashed upon me the idea of the survival of the fittest." Although Wallace was entirely unaware of it, this was essentially the same idea that had struck Darwin almost twenty years earlier.

In 1870, Wallace published *Contributions to the Theory of Natural Selection,* in which he described the ways that natural selection worked to provide through evolution certain physical features that benefited some creatures over others, such as the markings of their coats or the shape of their limbs. These principles applied to humans as well, of course, but when it came to the human mind, Wallace had a problem. He found himself unable to understand how the same physical processes could have yielded the self-awareness of human beings. Wallace's education and experience had disposed him to fit consciousness into a materialistic framework, but the longer he pondered the facts, the less convinced he became that mental states could be attributed solely to physical evolutionary forces.

In the caduceus, the emblem of the medical profession, the dove perched atop the snake-entwined staff has been interpreted as a symbol of the pineal gland poised over the spinal cord.

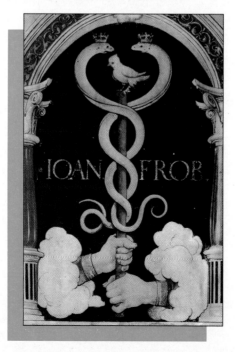

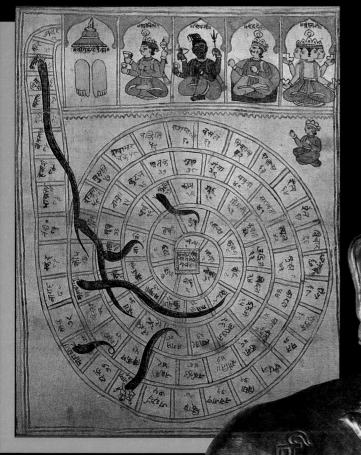

Golden lotus flowers inscribed with mystical signs blossom on the head and torso of this gleaming Indian sculpture. The symbols represent chakras, energy centers believed by the Hindus to be places where spirit and matter are joined. The seven chakras are thought to constitute the path to enlightenment. Indian mystics meditate on inspirational images, such as the one above, and follow physical regimens, such as yoga, to awaken the energy that brings the chakras to glowing life. In this manner, the mystics seek a state of awareness that transcends the limitations of mind and body.

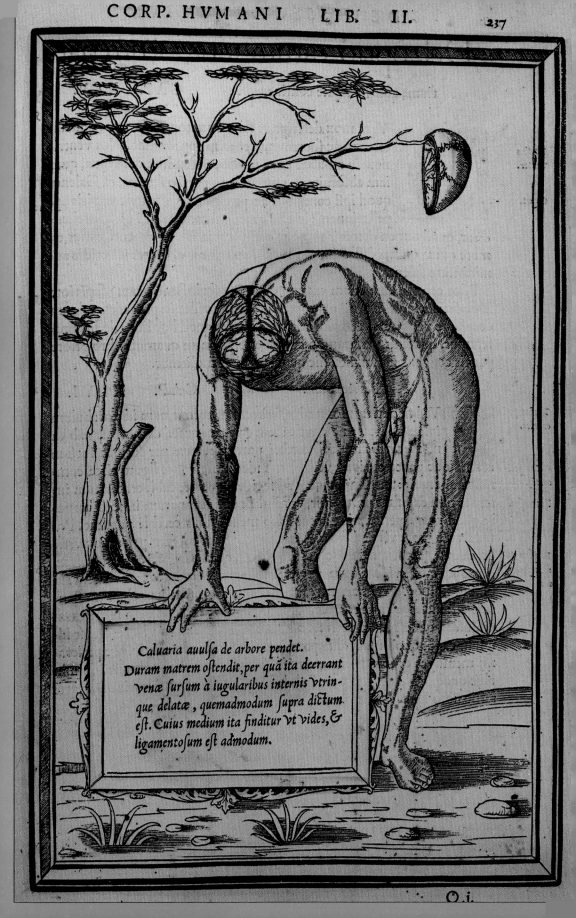

Caluaria auulſa de arbore pendet.
Duram matrem oſtendit, per quā ita deerrant
venæ ſurſum à iugularibus internis vtrin-
que delatæ, quemadmodum ſupra dictum.
eſt. Cuius medium ita finditur vt vides, &
ligamentoſum eſt admodum.

Several years before publishing his book on natural selection, Wallace had begun to attend spiritualist gatherings in England that were directed by well-known mediums of the day. At first, Wallace had no use for spiritual phenomena. But on a number of occasions he witnessed things that he, and many others, believed could not be scientifically explained. Victorian séances, for instance, produced startling displays: spirit rapping, in which sharp knocking sounds issued from tables without evident cause; levitation of people into the air by no visible means; and direct or automatic writing, in which messages appeared, seemingly spontaneously, on pieces of paper. Observing these alleged marvels, Wallace became fascinated by psychic phenomena, which he eventually concluded "are proved, quite as well as any facts are proved in other sciences."

From here it was a short step for Wallace to become convinced that the human mind "could not possibly have been developed by means of the same laws which have determined the progressive development of the organic world in general and also of man's physical organism." Instead, Wallace said, a metaphysical intervention must have taken place at two specific points in the course of human evolution to create consciousness: first to strike the initial spark of awareness in the humanoid brain and then again to spur the emergence of the first true civilizations.

Wallace pursued his investigations into the occult until his death in 1913. Although he was honored by the Order of Merit for his scientific researches in 1910, it is likely that his fame as a developer of the evolution theory was eroded in part by the derision some of his scientific peers heaped on his spiritualistic beliefs. Science, they declared, had no room for occult nonsense. Besides, for many scientists Wallace's misgivings about the evolution of consciousness had been rendered moot by a new point of view that emerged around the turn of the century.

By then, some brain researchers were proudly claiming to have solved the thorny issue bequeathed them by Huxley—that is, why consciousness should have evolved if it served no adaptive purpose. They proposed that consciousness was simply a property of matter that emerged when neurological systems became complex enough. These so-called emergent evolutionists pointed out that each successive unit of biochemical organization, from atom to molecule to cell and so on, exhibited properties that were not necessarily predictable from the behavior of their component parts. The wetness of the water molecule, for example, could not be logically derived from knowledge of the characteristics of the individual hydrogen and oxygen molecules composing it. Similarly, the metabolism of the cell was greater than the sum of its molecules. In this manner, emergent evolutionists made the case that consciousness could exhibit entirely different properties from the physical brain yet still be produced by it.

While some scientists wondered about the evolution of the mind, others began to take a more anatomical interest in mapping the terra incognita within the skull. Meticulous investigators dissected the brains of cadavers, microscopically examined brain tissues, analyzed and sketched neurons, and identified the ways in which the body's billions of nerve cells are knitted together to form the brain and nervous system. As the twentieth century waxed, the results of these investigations lent weight to the materialistic argument, which came into fullest flower in the mid-1950s with the hypothesis known as the mind-brain identity theory.

Identity theorists confirmed and extended the conviction of earlier materialists, namely that mental events are absolutely identical with neural events. That is, every thought or emotion a person experiences is generated by the electrochemical firing of neurons in the brain. The most ardent identity theorists contended that in time, science would pin open the mind in the way that anatomy students pinned open frogs or worms. When the underlying electrochemical patterns were drawn, it would be seen that each mental state corresponds to a particular pattern of physical activity. In short, they believed the mind to be nothing more than an ephemeral echo of the physical brain. In that sense, identity theorists said, mentation is no more mysterious than digestion. It is just an ordinary function of the healthy brain, and one need look no further than the strictly material realm to explain it.

The identity theory seemed enormously reasonable. It showed how a specific chain of events starting at the level of the cell and spreading by electrical signals along particular neuron networks of the nervous system could yield a specific mental state. And experiments had shown that a damaged brain can "learn" to use alternate neurological networks to produce that same mental state. For example, a person whose language center was damaged by a stroke might eventually speak again as different areas of the brain began to compensate for that one area's loss of function.

Even though the identity theory seems to offer a logical explanation of a complex process, according to some interested parties it does not address all aspects of the mind-brain debate. Australian physiologist Sir John Eccles contends that materialism's most firmly held article of faith, namely that neural events generate consciousness, simply begs the question. If all mental conditions are the result of physical neurological events, asks Eccles, how is it that the mental state thus engendered—say, anger—can in turn produce the physical effects on the body—such as increased blood pressure, tensed muscles, and internal temperature changes—that accompany anger?

Furthermore, he observes, materialism ignores the existence of such concepts as human will and free choice—forces that many of the world's religions and philosophies insist affect human behavior. The radical materialistic argument that mental events only appear to influence human behavior strikes Eccles, a former materialist turned dualist, as absurd. He insists that any theory of consciousness must deal with not only the brain's effect on the mind but also the mind's impact on the brain.

Eccles is far from alone in his criticism of strict materialism. While still upholding the spirit of the materialistic doctrine, some neuroscientists have identified qualities of the mind that defy reduction to the purely physical. Hungarian neuroscientist János Szentágothai, a dyed-in-the-wool materialist, is one such example. Over the course of his career, Szentágothai made key contributions to the study of the physiology of the central nervous system. In the 1970s he plunged into the philosophical issues surrounding consciousness. As a materialist, Szentágothai stated he could not imagine "any material (or non-material) substrate of my own inner self except the roughly 50 billion nerve cells" with their countless interconnections.

Yet at the same time, the Hungarian accepts that his mental "self" has the power to influence the activities of those thronging nerve cells in ways that are not yet understood. Somehow, Szentágothai suspects, the potential for consciousness is built into the essence of the brain cells. "I do not think," he writes, "that consciousness or even self-awareness starts with man. Its rudiments have to be there with the very existence of the 'neural.' " No neuroscientist, he states, "could claim that she or he completely

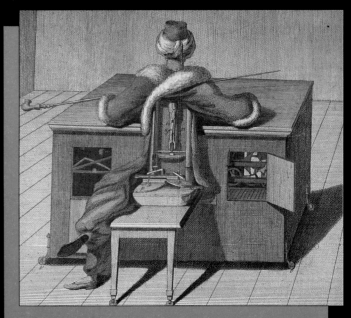

understands or can even correctly define the term mind."

In their search for answers to this dilemma, some disillusioned materialists have embraced a modified dualism. In a controversial 1977 book entitled *The Mind and Its Brain,* Eccles and his countryman, philosopher Sir Karl Popper, argue that in addition to brain states determined by physical laws, there are also mental states, which fall outside the boundaries of the material world yet interact with it. The authors posit three different worlds of reality and assert that what they call Worlds 2 and 3 should be considered every bit as real as World 1.

World 1 is the realm of physical objects, "of rocks and trees and physical fields of force." World 2 is the psychological realm, including the sensations produced by the senses—sight, sound, smell, taste, and touch—as well as thoughts, memories, dreams, imaginings, and other subjective experiences. Communication flows back and forth between Worlds 1 and 2 and results in World 3, the "products of the human mind": art, music, books, scientific theories—including, Popper adds wryly, "mistaken theories."

As a way of linking the worlds of physical and mental reality, Eccles, like Descartes, has located a place within the brain where the worlds of flesh and spirit interact. Descartes chose the pineal gland, but Eccles looked to a small tangle of nerves in the cerebral cortex named the supplementary motor area, or SMA. Experiments have shown that in the split second before an individual makes a voluntary movement—in the instant following a reader's mental decision to turn this page, say—a flurry of nerve impulses issue from the SMA. Eccles infers that this sudden surge of activity must be spawned by the arrival of signals from the nonmaterial mind.

Another significant experiment, by Danish neurophysiologist Per Roland, bolsters this inference. Roland showed that just before a light touch is applied to a finger of a subject who is watching the action, there is an increased flow of blood in the part of the brain that receives signals from the fingers. The increase, says Roland, must result from the subject's purely mental expectation of the touch—proof that mental activity produces physical activity.

Materialist holdouts argue that in suggesting the reality of a nonmaterial mind, Eccles and others have crossed into the territory of religion. In drawing the proper limits of their discipline, most scientists would agree in principle with the dictum of psychologist Donald Hebb. "The idea of an immaterial mind controlling the body is vitalism, no more, no less," he writes, "it has no place in science." Vitalism is the Aristotelian notion that a vital principle, or life force, flows in all living things—a theory that scientists have long denounced. Even Szentágothai, who admires the metaphorical power of Eccles and Popper's three-world model, maintains that to take the idea seriously "we should have to leave the domain of legitimate science and enter that of religion and faith."

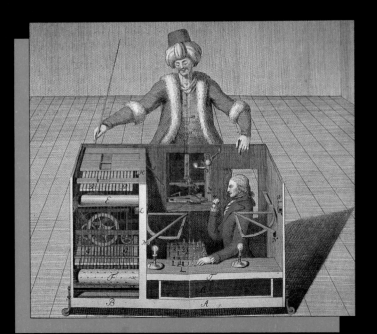

These eighteenth-century watercolors reveal the mechanical innards of the Phony Turk, a pipe-smoking, chess-playing automaton run by a man concealed beneath the robot's table. Some scientists and philosophers of the era concluded that the human mind was not qualitatively different from an automaton, since both were essentially machines. The only difference, said Frenchman Julien Offroy de La Mettrie, was that the mind was an "organic" machine rather than one constructed out of nuts and bolts.

Yet in allowing the possibility that the mind harbors a spiritual component, Eccles is in good historical company. For even while the materialists have vigorously pressed their case for the past 300 years, other scientists have less noisily taken the position that the exclusively materialistic description of the universe is shortsighted and that the explanation of a phenomenon in physical terms did not preclude its explanation in other terms. In other words, they have held the heretical position that science might not be the sole route to truth.

For example, the eighteenth-century German philosopher and mathematician Gottfried Wilhelm Leibniz, codiscoverer with Isaac Newton of calculus, suspected a metaphysical reality beyond the physical world. Space and time, mass, motion, and energy, Leibniz said, are merely intellectual constructs masking the underlying truth. William James, in his search to redefine consciousness, thought that the brain acted as a screen and filtered out a limited set of perceptions from a larger reality. Henri-Louis Bergson, an energetic and imaginative French philosopher who won a Nobel Prize for literature in 1928, agreed that the brain's main function was to pare down reality. That reality, he suggested, ultimately consisted of a "vital impulse" that could be grasped only by intuition.

Similarly, the eminent psychiatrist Carl Jung would not be bound by the physicists' strict definition of reality. In his monumental investigations of the mind, Jung paid particular attention to the zones just beyond the grasp of waking consciousness. Like Sigmund Freud, Jung expounded the importance of each human's unconscious mind, whose shadowy drives he believed shape behavior and yet are accessible to scrutiny only through creative outlets, such as dreams, fantasies, or artwork, and then only in symbolic terms. Jung's analysis of his own dreams and those of his colleagues and psychiatric patients led him to assert the existence of still another, broader type of unconscious, which he called the collective unconscious.

By Jung's reckoning, the collective unconscious belonged to all humankind. It was expressed in archetypes—or primitive symbols—myths, and folk tales with common themes and forms that could be found in every culture in every age. These potent images and stories, according to Jung, were not honed through individual experience but were the common inheritance of the species. In his writings, Jung sometimes endowed the collective unconscious with a paranormal power to foreshadow events. He believed, for instance, that a series of dreams he experienced toward the end of 1913, which were filled with images of flailing bodies drowning in seas of blood, presaged the global conflict that broke out in Europe the following year. In Jung's bold interpretations, the definition of the mind achieved a vast new dimension that transcended the scope of the materialist-dualist battle line.

Another farseeing Western effort to understand consciousness and eliminate the philosophical conflicts arising out of the classical dualistic and monistic ways of parsing the world was that of the renowned British mathematician and philosopher Alfred North Whitehead. One of Europe's leading thinkers in the years between the two world wars—and by all accounts a gentle and compassionate man—Whitehead created an elegant and formidable critique of reality called process philosophy. Although this difficult thesis defies paraphrasing, it holds, broadly, that space, time, and matter are intricately concocted abstractions, related to, but not equal to, reality. Whitehead saw reality, which is to say all that is, as being contrived from many interlocking fragments; no single aspect of reality could stand on its own. "There are no whole truths," wrote Whitehead, "all truths are half-truths. It is trying to treat them as whole truths that plays the devil."

Human consciousness consists principally of "actual entities," which are momentary experiences taking place in the present tense. These experiences derive from a category of "potentialities," the infinite set of all things that are, as well as of those things that "are not but might have been." The function of human consciousness is to grasp and unify as many actual entities as possible and transform them into

The fathers of evolutionary theory, Charles Darwin (left) and Alfred Russel Wallace (below), diverged in their views on the mind. Darwin argued that human mental capacities were the product of natural selection. His friend and colleague rejected this premise as "utterly inconceivable." Wallace asserted that there had to be a spiritual dimension to the mind that could not be explained by science. Darwin, in turn, was grieved by this appraisal, considering it a betrayal of their common hypothesis. He wrote to Wallace: "I hope you have not murdered too completely your own and my child."

memories, which, taken together, make up a person's sense of self. For Whitehead, the universe is constantly changing, and reality is a mesh of endless, interrelated transformations. ''Our minds are finite,'' wrote Whitehead, ''and yet even in these circumstances of finitude we are surrounded by possibilities that are infinite, and the purpose of human life is to grasp as much as we can out of that infinitude.''

In eschewing the mind-body split favored by Western dualism, Whitehead's difficult philosophy shows a striking similarity to certain aspects of Eastern thought and religion. For Buddhists, who freely acknowledge the metaphysical aspects of human consciousness, the analysis of human mentality has always involved a recognition of the central paradox of perception: The world of the body and objects, which appears so concrete, is illusory. True reality is accessible to contemplation but cannot be sounded by physical means. Nor can it be divided into subjects and objects, observers and things observed. Instead, true reality flows through the universe in an undifferentiated web.

An evocative illustration of this vision is found in the *Avatamsaka Sutra,* the Buddhist text set down sometime around the second or third century AD. The sutra describes a magical feature of the palace of Indra, the King of Heaven. Over the palace, the sutra reports, hangs a vast network of pearls so artfully arranged that by gazing at any one of the pearls, a viewer is able simultaneously to see the reflections of all the others. To interpreters of Buddhist thought, Indra's cleverly configured net symbolizes the spiritual interconnectedness of all things in the infinite universe.

The teachings of Hinduism also extol the existence of a truth beyond immediate perception that is similar to the Buddhist dharmakaya, the melding of the mind and the material world. The Hindus call it Brahman, the essence of the universe. It is impersonal and dimensionless, although it fills space. It is basically inaccessible to human awareness,

*"Wholly unconscious of what it meant,"
Swiss psychiatrist Carl Jung painted his first
mandala (above) in 1916. He later concluded that such "magic circles" were instinctive
renderings of a universal symbol that people
have been drawing for 20,000 years. Creating mandalas, he wrote, tapped directly into
"the microcosmic nature of the psyche,"
bringing to light an individual's repressed
and forgotten life experiences. He considered the process so enlightening that he
made painting and interpreting mandalas
part of his treatment for many patients.*

23

Albin MICHEL
ÉDITEUR
22, rue Huyghens, 22
PARIS (14e)

LE PETIT INVENTEUR

ABONNEMENTS :
FRANCE...... **12** francs
ÉTRANGER.. **18** francs

LES ONDES HUMAINES

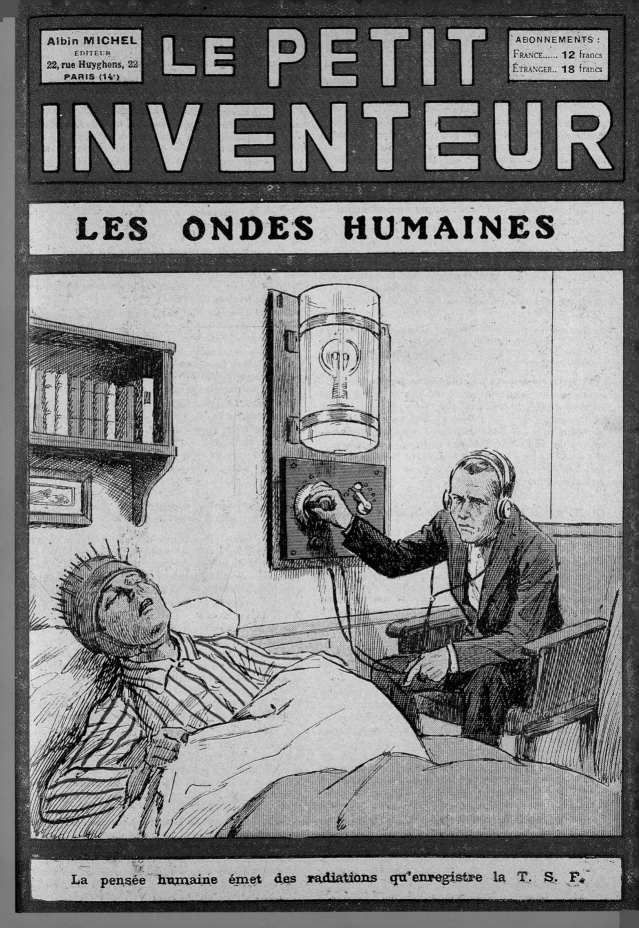

La pensée humaine émet des radiations qu'enregistre la T. S. F.

which is blinded by the mind's built-in tendency to compartmentalize, categorize, name, and reason. These mental qualities, Hindus believe, separate the mind from the undifferentiated Brahman.

The great Eastern philosophy called Taoism admits the truth of the objective world while also proclaiming a holistic view. In exploring the nature of consciousness and of the universe, Taoism emphasizes that the world of appearances is complemented by another world, one of non-being, and that behind these two worlds lies an even deeper reality called the Tao. It is an elusive concept that can be grasped only by indirection or paradox. The eternal Tao is constantly in flux, and its followers must be in tune with its unpredictable flow. The enlightened person, says the basic text of Taoism, the *Tao-te ching,* will "Act without action. Do without ado." He or she understands that "To yield is to be preserved whole. To be bent is to become straight. To be empty is to be full. To be worn out is to be renewed."

Despite their mystical aspects, the Buddhist, Hindu, and Taoist views of consciousness and the cosmos show astonishing parallels to the new vision of the universe unveiled by the investigations of twentieth-century physicists. Fritjof Capra was among the first Western scientists to explore the implausible parallels between ancient mysticism and modern physics. In 1975 he wrote in *The Tao of Physics,* "The basic oneness of the universe is not only the central characteristic of the mystical experience, but is also one of the most important revelations of modern physics. It becomes apparent at the atomic level and manifests itself more and more as one penetrates deeper into matter, down into the realm of subatomic particles."

The principal architects of modern physics were Albert Einstein and Niels Bohr, who succeeded in overthrowing classical Newtonian physics as it applied both to the very large and to the very small. Newton's solid and predictable universe had come to be replaced by a far more tenuous and quirky cosmos. In the early decades of the twentieth century, Einstein showed that energy and matter were simply different forms of the same thing, which could be translated into one or the other form in calculable proportions. In his theories, Einstein revealed that space and time were also inextricably related, and he argued that the size of any object or the duration of any event was relative, depending entirely on where the observer stood.

Meanwhile, Niels Bohr and German physicist Werner Heisenberg eyed the atom and discovered that it was less substantial than earlier physicists had supposed. It was impossible, they showed mathematically, to calculate with any certainty where in a given atom a particular electron would be at a given moment. Instead, an electron's position could be stated only in terms of probabilities, as a matter of the likelihood that it would be in a certain place at a certain time.

So slippery is the footing on the playground of quantum physics, in fact, that some scientists have had to conclude that the very presence of human consciousness affects the train of events on the subatomic level. Indeed, it appears that human perception, having the power to change reality by observing it, constitutes an integral part of the universe. In describing the quantum universe's interconnected web, of which human consciousness is a part, Capra wrote, "None of the properties of any part of this web is fundamental; they all follow from the properties of the other parts, and the overall consistency of their mutual interrelations determines the structure of the entire web."

In noting the paradoxical confluence of ancient mysticism and modern physics, German theologian and philosopher Rudolph Otto drew an intriguing correlation. He suggested that the urge to find out about the world—the motivating force for a scientist—is rooted in the mystical intuition that a oneness lies behind the physical world's multiplicity. Now, it seems, after centuries of pursuing divergent paths, the methods of the mystic and the scientist are converging.

If the universe is nondeterministic, as modern physics claims, and if all nature flows through an interpenetrating web, then there is no basis for the classical divisions of ob-

Neurosurgeon Wilder Penfield came to doubt that the mind would ever be understood purely through study of the brain. He illustrated this view with a rock painting in which a broken line links the Greek word for spirit with the symbols of science and the brain.

the new science of holography, a method of creating images using lasers. To form an image, light from the laser is split into two beams. One beam is directed toward the object to be photographed and the other is aimed toward a mirror. Both beams then reflect onto a photosensitive plate or film, which produces a chaotic-looking mass of light and dark swirls. Although this pattern appears confused when viewed with the naked eye, a stunning transformation takes place when the hologram is illuminated by a laser beam: An image appears of the object photographed that remains convincingly three-dimensional when viewed from different angles. A further, significant attribute of a hologram is that each small bit of holographic film contains virtually the same information as the whole. If a hologram on a photographic plate were to shatter, the entire image could be reconstituted from even a square centimeter of the original.

Pribram's studies convinced him that the brain stored information in much the same way, that is, not in specific spatial division but distributed over the entire neural network. Human brains, he proposes, exhibit the same properties as holograms, not only in creating a three-dimensional version of the world from electrochemical impulses from the senses but also in spreading information across the entire system, so that even if portions of the brain are damaged, the functions performed by those parts of the brain or the memories stored there are preserved.

But, having decided the brain was a hologram, Pribram was stymied, because his model still left him asking who was looking at the hologram, reconstituting it, as it were, into three dimensions. Pribram puzzled over this problem and concluded that he must be asking the wrong question. Perhaps there *was* no objective world that was being rebuilt in the brain. Perhaps the universe itself was also holographic and the "lenses" of the senses were, like a reconstituting laser beam, endowing it with a ghostly yet convincing dimensionality. Excited by this conjecture, Pribram by chance learned of the musings of physicist David Bohm, who had made a rather convincing case for the holographic organization of the universe.

ject and subject, mind and body. The insights of the new physics demand a more holistic view of consciousness, and some daring thinkers have attempted to forge a bold, synthetic vision of human awareness. One of the most exciting holistic hypotheses to emerge in recent years is that advanced by two Americans, neuroscientist Karl Pribram, who heads Radford University's Center for Brain Research and Information Sciences in Radford, Virginia, and physicist David Bohm, emeritus professor of theoretical physics at Birkbeck College, University of London.

Like so many others, Pribram began his career as a strict materialist in the 1940s but gradually accepted the idea that the mind might be more than the product of brain activity. He became intrigued with a concept suggested by

Bohm argued that the deep reality of the universe is enfolded, invisible to observation by classical scientific means. Through mathematical modeling and analogy, Bohm had glimpsed a reality akin to the Eastern concepts of dharmakaya, Brahman, or Tao; as he put it, an "intangible, invisible flux" of "inseparable interconnectedness." To Bohm, the idea of a stable world of normal consciousness was an illusion. The universe, in his estimation, was kaleidoscopic and dynamic, in a state of being that he dubbed the "holomovement."

Pribram took the critical step of fusing his idea of the holographic mind with Bohm's holographic universe and created a theory of consciousness with metaphysical implications, boldly bridging the moat between science and religion. Pribram proposed that classical thinkers had been misguided in trying to sort out the differences between mind and body; as the mystics proclaimed, belief in such a split was delusive. Consciousness, Pribram said, was an extension of the larger, hidden reality. Mental properties were not an anomalous, ineffable part of the material world; they were, he wrote in a 1978 essay titled "What the Fuss Is All About," the "pervasive organizing principles of the universe, which includes the brain."

Pribram's theory brings Western thinking close indeed to Eastern mysticism, dissolving distinctions between mental and physical, spiritual and material. In the holographic domain, Pribram explains, "What is organism (with its component organs) is no longer sharply distinguished from what lies outside the boundaries of the skin. In the holographic domain, each organism represents in some manner the universe, and each portion of the universe represents in some manner the organisms within it."

In 1949 Jorge Luis Borges, the brilliant, blind, Argentine writer, published a short story called "The Aleph." The tale describes a narrator's discovery, in the basement of a house in Buenos Aires, of the magical Aleph, "one of the points in space that contains all of the other points."

More than a geometric or optical oddity, the imaginary Aleph, measuring about an inch in diameter, turns out to be a window into the boundless, ever-changing universe. Through it the awe-struck narrator viewed, "in a single gigantic instant," everything that has ever happened or will happen. Past, present, and future "occupied the same point in space, without overlapping or transparency." Grappling to recount what he saw, the narrator then lists in series the impressions that had in fact rushed simultaneously into his consciousness:

"Each thing (a mirror's face, let's say) was infinite things, since I distinctly saw it from every angle of the universe. I saw the teeming sea; I saw daybreak and nightfall; I saw the multitudes of America; I saw a silvery cobweb in the center of a black pyramid; I saw a splintered labyrinth (it was London). . . . I saw bunches of grapes, snow, tobacco, lodes of metal, steam; I saw convex equatorial deserts and each one of their grains of sand; I saw a woman in Inverness whom I shall never forget. . . . I saw a sunset in Querétaro that seemed to reflect the color of a rose in Bengal. . . . I saw horses with flowing manes on a shore of the Caspian Sea at dawn; I saw the delicate bone structure of a hand. . . . I saw in a showcase in Mirzapur a pack of Spanish playing cards; I saw the slanting shadows of ferns on a greenhouse floor; I saw tigers, pistons, bisons, tides, and armies; I saw all the ants on the planet. . . . I saw the circulation of my own dark blood. . . . and I felt dizzy and wept, for my eyes had seen that secret and conjectured object whose name is common to all men but which no man has looked upon—the unimaginable universe."

In a fictional frame, Borges's story seems to blend parts of Bohm's and Pribram's holographic visions of universe and mind, which were not developed until later, as well as the old Eastern mystics' notion of Indra's fabulous reflecting pearls. It is almost as if all these disparate consciousnesses were themselves peering into a hologram—viewing an image of which, in turn, they were each a part. Perhaps in this mutual mirroring of art, science, and mysticism there glimmers a hint of understanding of that most puzzling of entities, the human mind.

Seeing Clues in an Unseen Light

The aura is the weathervane of the soul," wrote American psychic Edgar Cayce. Like others over the years, Cayce declared that he could actually perceive the aura, said to be a three-dimensional nimbus of glowing colored energy emanating from every living thing, plant or animal. Believers in the aura say that it provides insight into an individual's health, emotions, and psychological attitudes—or, as Cayce put it, "the way the winds of destiny are blowing" for that person.

Doctors in ancient Persia purportedly diagnosed physical illness by studying the light they discerned surrounding their patients. Sixteenth-century Swiss physician and alchemist Paracelsus wrote that he observed signs of health or disease in the "luminous sphere" radiating from human beings. Today, aura interpreters report that both mental and physical problems manifest themselves in the body's swathe of colored light. Others find clues to spiritual development, believing that a brilliant aura reflects an enlightened being. Modern enthusiasts argue that the halos of holy figures in old paintings are not simply artistic conventions, but auras. Contemporary aura readers tell of bright light enveloping people who are in harmony with themselves and the world.

The following pages reveal a system of interpretation developed by Barbara Bowers of San Diego, a self-described aura consultant. Her method focuses on personality and individual potential. Moreover, according to Bowers, it can also tell you the color of your own aura—and what it means.

Yellow and Physical Tan constitute the physical (body) family of personality colors. Bowers says people with these colors take cues about the world from their bodies. Before they consider a situation intellectually or respond to it emotionally, they experience a physical reaction such as sweaty palms, increased heart rate, or nervous fidgeting.

Red, Orange, and Magenta make up the physical (environment) family of personality colors. People in this group experience life as physical reality. In order to grapple with an idea, they must be able to give it tangible form. According to Barbara Bowers, action is crucial to these individuals, and they live with "gusto, verve, and courage."

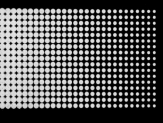

YELLOW
Yellows have the most childlike personalities of all, Bowers says. Sociable, active, and fun-loving, they revel in physical joys. But their bodies are highly sensitive to pain, sometimes causing them to fall prey to physical addictions in their efforts to soothe themselves.

PHYSICAL TAN
Physical Tans are the enigmas of the spectrum. Silent and inward turning, they tend to be rigid thinkers with little ability to share their feelings with others, let alone with themselves. When they do open up, however, their intimacy is particularly intense.

RED
Literal-minded, hardworking, and generous, Reds are pragmatists who thrive when tasks require physical prowess. They love nature, deal with feelings straightforwardly, and are usually optimistic. But their explosive tempers make them potentially violent.

ORANGE
Oranges "shake their fists in the face of God," Bowers says. Their daredevil existence revolves around one life-and-death challenge after another, leaving little time for relationships or other forms of personal development.

MAGENTA
Magentas are nonconformists. Individualistic rather than rebellious, they burgeon with an offbeat creativity that seems bizarre to some. Bowers advises them to resist temptations to hide their differences: Their uniqueness is the source of their identity.

Like Edgar Cayce and many others who have claimed to see auras, Barbara Bowers says that throughout her childhood she assumed that everyone perceived the bands of color surrounding human bodies. After years of seeing auras, she decided to explain her system of interpretation in her book, What Color Is Your Aura?

Five of the fourteen types of personality bands that Bowers claims to perceive are unusual hues or color combinations to which she has attached special names. Mental Tan, a rich honey gold, is so called to distinguish it from three double colors that also have "tan" in their names. Physical Tan, Nurturing Tan, and Loving Tan are each made up of a band of Mental Tan immediately surrounding the body and a second ring of color—green, blue, or red, respectively—outside the tan. Crystal, the fifth unusual color, is "a gossamer, foglike mist with other colors in it."

Descriptions of the personality colors—which Bowers groups by similar traits into four families—appear below. To find out what yours is, see pages 36 and 37.

MENTAL FAMILY

A personality color from the mental family is said to signify a cerebral approach to the world. Individuals who fall into this category think tirelessly and perceive reality through thoughts and ideas, which they love to play with and organize. Their greatest challenge in life is attempting to handle the seeming irrationality of emotion.

MENTAL TAN
Logical thinking is the hallmark of the Mental Tans. Their humming minds operate methodically. They may seem pedantic to others, says Bowers, while they themselves may be perplexed and disturbed by their feelings, which exist outside their intellectual bailiwick.

GREEN
With their razor-sharp, analytical minds, Greens often leave others in the dust of their fast-paced creativity. They strive for perfection out of fear of inadequacy. Their happiness depends on voluminous productivity; Bowers says they see life as "a giant 'to do' list."

NURTURING TAN
Nurturing Tans are the good samaritans of the world, offering others emotional support, physical aid, and altruistic kindness. They marry a dedication to humanity with acute intelligence, a pairing that produces concrete results.

LOVING TAN
Loving Tans feel a deep love for humanity. Yet they hesitate to carry this affection to a personal level: Since childhood, most have been rejected because of their maddening disorganization.

EMOTIONAL/SPIRITUAL FAMILY

People whose personality colors fall in the emotional/spiritual family prefer hopes, wishes, and dreams to tangible reality. They value emotions as well as feelings and perform at their peak when they are able to rely upon intuition rather than upon logic. In their ephemeral realm, "abstraction has more reality than does paying the bills."

BLUE
Blues live to serve others. However, they approach life purely emotionally, guided by their keen intuition. Logical thought processes confuse them, and they have trouble making decisions. Further, they lack the assertiveness to ask that their own needs be met.

VIOLET
Passionate and somewhat egotistical, Violets possess the intelligence and intuition required to "make a significant difference" in the world. Guilt and fear sometimes hinder their quest for achievement, but ultimately they are able to realize their dreams.

LAVENDER
Bowers says Lavenders seem always to be suffering from "a kind of jet lag." Caught between their own fantasy worlds and the intrusive demands of the real world, they are open to paranormal experiences. Their rich daydreams fuel magical artistic creations.

CRYSTAL
Directly linked to a higher power, Crystals have special healing powers, Bowers reports. Despite this divine connection, they find the world harsh and cold. They have no instinct about social behavior, so they copy peers, actually adopting other colors into their auras.

INDIGO
According to Bowers, Indigo appeared as a personality color only recently. She says these children and young adults will become the leaders of a new age because they were born with an innate omniscience. They are free of the problems that plague other people.

Insights from the Outer Bands

The mantle of colored light that allegedly surrounds human beings extends far beyond the personality color. In addition to that primary layer, the aura boasts five to seven others. These outer bands vary in number and color over the course of life, and they disclose information about events, feelings, and priorities.

Bowers divides what she calls the auric bands into three groups. The first contains the personality color, what she dubs an overlay, if there is one, and a spirituality band. The overlay is a second personality color that may radiate around the head and shoulders outside the primary band. It adds another group of characteristics—which may be quite different from the first—to the mix of an individual's personality. Outside that is the spirituality band, consisting of a white space, the width of which reveals the degree of a person's spiritual growth.

Bowers calls the second group the drive bands. These layers, three or four in number, show resentment or contentment with some aspect of one's life. They may also refer to the planning or execution of projects or to the status of a personal goal.

The outermost layers of the aura are called the power bands. They express a person's way of handling authority. The first band in this group is usually red and indicates by its size and by the depth of its color how a person was treated early in life. The second layer sheds light upon how one leads others, and the final band divulges an individual's feelings about romantic relationships.

Colors that frequently emerge in the outer bands and the meanings that Bowers ascribes to them appear at right.

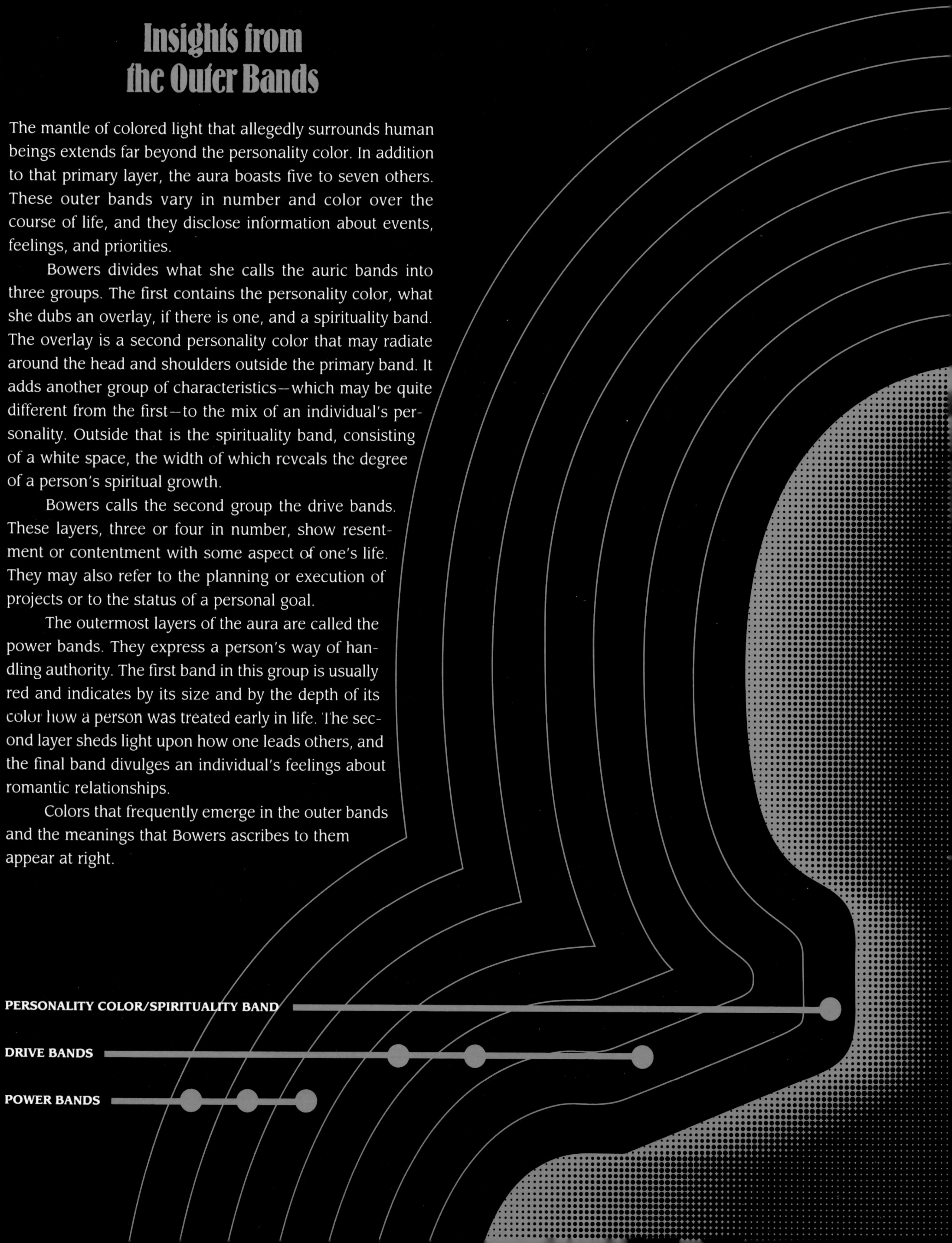

PERSONALITY COLOR/SPIRITUALITY BAND

DRIVE BANDS

POWER BANDS

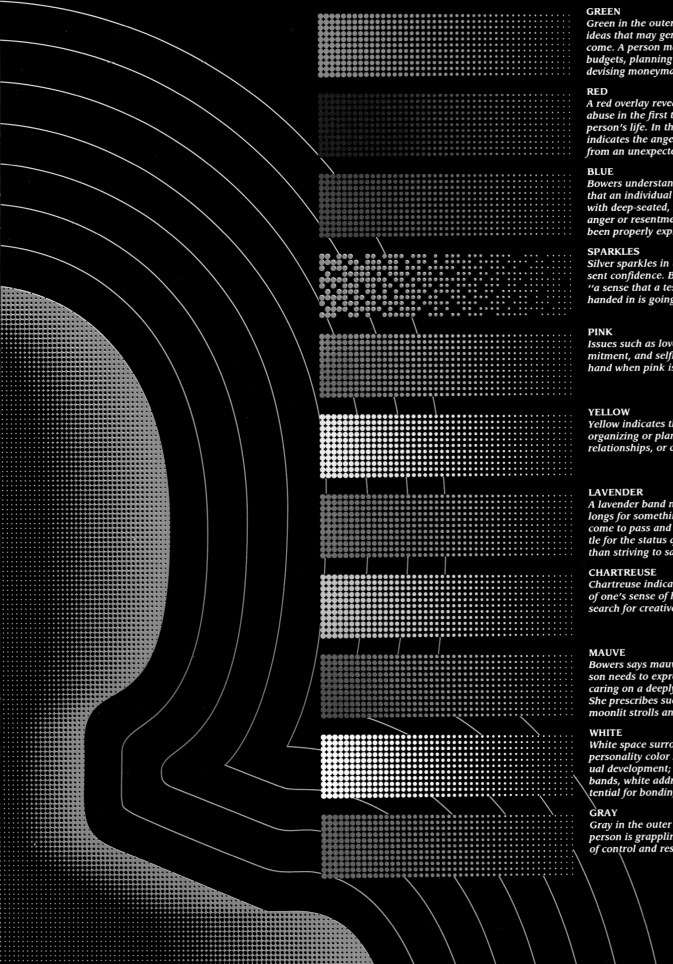

GREEN
Green in the outer layers suggests ideas that may generate new income. A person may be revising budgets, planning finances, or devising moneymaking schemes.

RED
A red overlay reveals trauma or abuse in the first three years of a person's life. In the drive bands, it indicates the anger that results from an unexpected turn of events.

BLUE
Bowers understands blue to mean that an individual is contending with deep-seated, longstanding anger or resentment that has not been properly expressed.

SPARKLES
Silver sparkles in the aura represent confidence. Bowers describes "a sense that a test you just handed in is going to be an A."

PINK
Issues such as love, family, commitment, and selfless giving are at hand when pink is in the aura.

YELLOW
Yellow indicates that a person is organizing or planning for jobs, relationships, or creative pursuits.

LAVENDER
A lavender band means a person longs for something that will never come to pass and chooses to settle for the status quo rather than striving to satisfy the desires.

CHARTREUSE
Chartreuse indicates the discovery of one's sense of humor and the search for creative outlets for it.

MAUVE
Bowers says mauve signals a person needs to express closeness and caring on a deeply personal level. She prescribes such pleasures as moonlit strolls and soft music.

WHITE
White space surrounding the personality color indicates spiritual development; in the power bands, white addresses one's potential for bonding with children.

GRAY
Gray in the outer layers signals a person is grappling with the issues of control and responsibility.

A Sampler of the Aura Reader at Work

Barbara Bowers believes that many children perceive auras but that they usually drop the gift because their elders reprimand them for reporting the phenomenon. Even as adults, she says, some people possess an untapped visual sensitivity to the nimbus. She advises, however, that no one read an aura without careful consideration: Serious issues that beginners may not know how to handle sometimes surface.

Bowers says she sees auras by using her peripheral vision. She begins by reading the bands closest to the body—believing them to contain the most salient information—then moves outward. She says the aura has texture, sound, size, shape, and color, which contribute to her understanding. Four of her readings appear below, with silhouettes representing the people she studied.

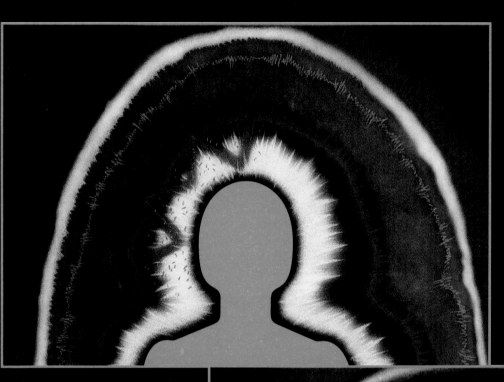

The aura Bowers sees around a twenty-seven-year-old male reveals he is a fun-loving Yellow. The gray jags over his right shoulder declare heterosexuality, and the pink band encircling the yellow suggests a new romance. The chartreuse band means he is opening himself to genuine joy and laughter for the first time in years, although he does not fully trust this instinct yet, as the faintness of the color relates. The blue band divulges his anger against a demanding parent, feeling he has spent too much of his life trying to live up to another's expectations. Bowers counsels that he should express these sentiments—if only to himself—since she believes that unresolved resentment can produce illness. The dark red line encircles the man's body, showing that just one of his parents nurtured him. The white band indicates he is not ready to bond with children. And the band of pink discloses that he is open to intimate relationships but still has many things to learn before marriage.

An iconoclastic Magenta, the thirty-five-year-old woman whose aura appears at right experienced trauma early in life, says Bowers. A red overlay reveals that the pain she suffered during a difficult birth has made her defensive, and the red streak betrays a recent argument. The rich yellow suggests that the woman is working on a creative project. The deep pink band tells that people have criticized her for her unabashed expression of her sexuality, and this has shaken her self-esteem, as the gray band signals. She doubts her ability to make money, according to the faint green band, but she need not: The darker green outline ensures her success. The smooth red line reveals her parents' laissez-faire attitude about her upbringing. And the white band indicates she is not ready for children. The darker edge of pink divulges that this strongly individualistic woman will have trouble forming an emotional bond with those who try to confine her.

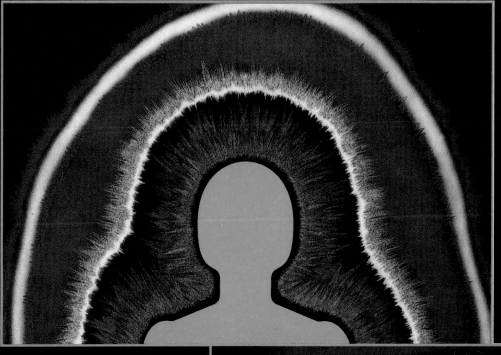

The green personality color and violet overlay in the aura of another mid-thirties female, Bowers declares, reveal that she has an agile mind broadened by a visionary nature. The tightly defined nature of these bands symbolizes that she has felt restricted by loved ones throughout her life. The narrowness of the white band between the overlay and the drive bands suggests that she has not yet realized her spiritual potential. The thin yellow band divulges her nascent creativity, and its close pairing with the surrounding moss green shows that it may earn her money. The wide band of lavender indicates melancholy. Bowers linked it to a frustration in the woman's relationship with her boyfriend. The jagged red band tells that the woman's mother did not provide the kind of support her daughter needed. And the thinness of the outermost band, which relates to love, again points up concerns the woman faces with her boyfriend.

A fifty-eight-year-old man whose aura appears at right is a visionary Violet. The broad white band between the violet and the next color indicates that he has pondered his spirituality deeply. The fluffy lavender suggests an impatience about his artistic vision, which is as yet unfulfilled. His timely and original creativity shines from the yellow stripes, as his professional confidence does from the silver sparkles: He knows his work is good. The red band is quite thin and dark, showing that he is no longer influenced by his upbringing. The pink relationship band is marked off by a boundary line, which means that the man's marriage has reached a limit beyond which further growth may be impossible. Bowers counsels that he may either leave the relationship or may seek from friends the support and stimulation that he does not receive from his wife. Maintaining the current state of the marriage, she says, will thwart the realization of his vision.

What Color Is Your Aura?

Barbara Bowers developed the questionnaire below to help people who cannot see the aura identify their personality color. The ninety-eight short statements are divided into fourteen groups—the fourteen personality colors. The group in which you score the highest (thirty-five is the highest possible) determines yours.

Before beginning the test, read each of the five responses carefully. They are:

1 This does NOT describe me.

2 I am VERY SELDOM like this.

3 SOMETIMES I am like this.

4 I am OFTEN like this.

5 This is ME!

To begin the test, use a piece of paper to cover the colors that appear at the end of each of the fourteen rows of answer spaces. This way, your responses will not be influenced by what you already know about each personality color. Respond to each statement quickly, writing the number of your response in the appropriate answer space. Do not linger over the choices. If you have difficulty responding to a statement, your answer is probably "1" or "2."

After you complete the test, find the colors in which you have scored the highest by adding the numbers in each row of answer spaces. Go back to the groups of statements that apply to those colors and respond to each again, this time giving them more thought. Compute your scores a second time to determine your true personality color. A second significantly high score reveals that you have an overlay in addition to your main color. Keep in mind that each color has its inherent strengths and that no color is better than another.

THE QUESTIONNAIRE

1. You are methodical in your thinking.

2. You have a strong inner desire to make your mark on the world.

3. You resent emotional and domestic demands made on you.

4. Esoteric spiritual or political philosophies have great emotional and intellectual appeal for you.

5. You seek the unusual or the avant-garde.

6. You cry easily.

7. You are not judgmental or critical of the ways in which others express their emotions or feelings.

8. You are at ease in any environment where healing is the primary activity or occupation.

9. When faced with a dangerous task, you carefully plan how to handle any crisis that may arise.

10. You are a loner.

11. When solving problems, you are able to visualize all the steps and the solution at the same time.

12. You have no biases about sexuality—heterosexuality, bisexuality, or homosexuality.

13. You prefer working at jobs that are physically demanding.

14. You react physically (with sweaty palms, for example) before you respond to a situation mentally or emotionally.

15. As a leader, you solicit lots of detailed information from others in order to make decisions.

16. Social get-togethers such as cocktail parties bore you.

17. You prefer occupations that have unlimited financial opportunity, such as sales.

18. When you have money, you spend it; when you don't, you don't.

19. You are a nonconformist.

20. You have a hard time saying no when people ask you to do them a favor.

21. You organize projects by creating systems.

22. You depend on other people for clues on how you should act in various social situations.

23. You meet physical challenges without fear.

24. You are slow to choose friends.

25. You do not require emotional loyalty to effectively mentor someone.

26. In school, you learn most effectively in an unstructured environment.

27. For you, sex is for physical pleasure.

28. When you find yourself in a tense situation, you want to run away or pretend it does not exist.

29. You have difficulty sharing your emotions and feelings with others.

30. You would rather be the theorist of a project, and leave the building of the working model to someone else.

31. You diagnose problems by recognizing patterns.

32. You are a dreamer who likes to live in the fantasies you create.

33. You are a spontaneous person.

34. The experience of God's love is the spiritual force in your life.

35. You look for ways to improve your community.

36. You rarely show your deepest feelings.

37. You prefer activities that allow you to demonstrate physical prowess.

38. You evaluate objects by how solid or substantial they feel.

39. You are attracted to religions with strong theological structures that allow for personal interpretation.

40. You lead by forcing others to rethink and reexamine old beliefs, values, and ways of doing things.

41. When you lose your temper, you get over it quickly.

42. You are not cynical.

43. You like social activities that combine business and pleasure.

44. You are not "free and easy" when spending your money on others.

45. You see God as the "brain" that created the universe.

46. You express your sexuality creatively, intuitively, and experimentally.

47. You are attracted to products that have unusual or unexpected design features.

48. When looking for a job, you have difficulty asking for the salary you deserve.

49. You feel that raising a well-educated child is the greatest contribution you can make to your community.

50. You enjoy reading biographies and diaries that describe the lives of real people.

51. *You prefer individual competition rather than team effort.*

52. *You are slow to commit to any belief system.*

53. *You eagerly seek to please those you love and care about.*

54. *You perceive spirituality to be in everything you do.*

55. *If you have enough money to buy the necessities, you are happy.*

56. *You experience God as the physical sensation of the joy of being alive.*

57. *You prefer a spiritual belief system that relies on a foundation of laws and principles.*

58. *You lead by telling people what to do.*

59. *You prefer a few specially chosen friends who stimulate you intellectually.*

60. *Your artistic pursuits often keep you indoors.*

61. *You form loose friendships that are not encumbered with bonds of expectation.*

62. *You feel more comfortable sharing the leadership by being a co-chairperson.*

63. *You financially support community groups and programs that benefit society.*

64. *Your source of personal power is your ability to mentally retreat inward.*

65. *You are not interested in organized religion or other belief systems.*

66. *You are meticulous in following instructions given to you by your supervisor.*

67. *You prefer social gatherings where you have an opportunity to talk to many different people.*

68. *You need to be awakened slowly from a sound sleep to avoid being irritable or in physical pain.*

69. *When playing a team sport, you rally the team when the chips are down.*

70. *You like parties.*

71. *To you, money is security.*

72. *You feel compelled to do something significant with your life.*

73. *You find great satisfaction in assisting people by giving ideas and information.*

74. *You prefer a somewhat isolated existence rather than one in which you would have to conform to society's expectations.*

75. *When you see something that you like, you choose to have your fantasy now and pay later.*

76. *You do not enjoy endurance sports such as cross-country skiing or weight-lifting.*

77. *You feel that spiritual principles must have practical application in the real world.*

78. *You prefer quiet, introspective, spiritual disciplines.*

79. *You prefer to work for a commission, or even as a freelancer, rather than for a regular, fixed salary.*

80. *You believe that to be a good leader, you must first be a good follower.*

81. *You have difficulty managing money effectively.*

82. *You cannot be coerced into doing something in which you are not interested.*

83. *You experience spirituality when you physically participate in the worship service.*

84. *You lead others with enthusiasm because you enjoy being with people.*

85. *You enjoy working with mechanical devices such as computers, calculators, and stereo equipment.*

86. *Possessions are important to you as stepping-stones to power and influence.*

87. *To you, ideas are things, not mental abstractions.*

88. *You see ideas as three-dimensional patterns.*

89. *You express your spirituality through your strong connection with nature.*

90. *When making a decision, you try to find a solution that will please everyone.*

91. *You lead others by incorporating their feelings into the decision-making process.*

92. *You work best in an environment that is calm and peaceful with limited contact with others.*

93. *You do not need friends or social interaction to be happy.*

94. *To you, money represents physical safety and stability.*

95. *You have difficulty keeping track of personal possessions.*

96. *You are content to work with your hands.*

97. *You want to know how and why things work the way they do.*

98. *You enjoy working in occupations that require physical activity.*

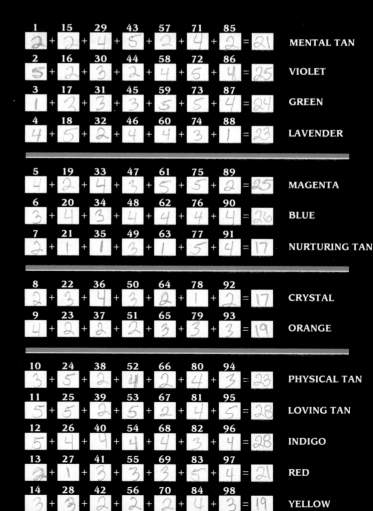

1	15	29	43	57	71	85		
2 +	2 +	4 +	5 +	2 +	4 +	2	= 21	MENTAL TAN

2	16	30	44	58	72	86		
5 +	2 +	3 +	2 +	4 +	5 +	4	= 25	VIOLET

3	17	31	45	59	73	87		
1 +	2 +	3 +	3 +	5 +	5 +	4	= 24	GREEN

4	18	32	46	60	74	88		
4 +	5 +	2 +	4 +	4 +	3 +	1	= 23	LAVENDER

5	19	33	47	61	75	89		
4 +	2 +	4 +	3 +	5 +	5 +	2	= 25	MAGENTA

6	20	34	48	62	76	90		
3 +	4 +	3 +	4 +	4 +	4 +	4	= 26	BLUE

7	21	35	49	63	77	91		
2 +	1 +	1 +	3 +	1 +	5 +	4	= 17	NURTURING TAN

8	22	36	50	64	78	92		
2 +	3 +	4 +	3 +	2 +	1 +	2	= 17	CRYSTAL

9	23	37	51	65	79	93		
4 +	2 +	2 +	2 +	3 +	3 +	3	= 19	ORANGE

10	24	38	52	66	80	94		
3 +	5 +	2 +	4 +	2 +	4 +	3	= 23	PHYSICAL TAN

11	25	39	53	67	81	95		
5 +	5 +	2 +	5 +	2 +	4 +	5	= 28	LOVING TAN

12	26	40	54	68	82	96		
5 +	4 +	4 +	4 +	4 +	3 +	4	= 28	INDIGO

13	27	41	55	69	83	97		
2 +	1 +	3 +	3 +	3 +	5 +	4	= 21	RED

14	28	42	56	70	84	98		
3 +	3 +	2 +	2 +	2 +	4 +	3	= 19	YELLOW

CHAPTER 2

Windows into the Brain

Diagnosed at various times in their lives as severely retarded, autistic, or psychotic, identical twins George and Charles might elicit little more than mild curiosity or even a momentary feeling of aversion from a stranger meeting them for the first time. In his 1987 book, *The Man Who Mistook His Wife for a Hat,* neurologist Oliver Sacks notes that the twins are "unprepossessing at first encounter—a sort of grotesque Tweedledum and Tweedledee . . . undersized, with disturbing disproportions in head and hands, high-arched palates, high-arched feet, monotonous squeaky voices, a variety of peculiar tics and mannerisms, and a very high generative myopia, requiring glasses so thick that their eyes seem distorted, giving them the appearance of absurd little professors." Professors they could never be, however. Though by then middle-aged—they were born in 1939—the twins had IQs that measured between sixty and seventy, equivalent to that of an eight- to ten-year-old child. They can read only a few simple words and must struggle to do even the most rudimentary addition and subtraction problems with any accuracy. The concepts of multiplication and division are entirely beyond their comprehension. When asked the product of seven times four, one of the twins replied, "two." When asked what seven times four meant, he answered, "It means fourteen."

Despite their physical and mental limitations, though, the twins possess some truly remarkable abilities. They can memorize 300-digit numbers with ease and often play a game together in which they exchange 8-, 9-, and even 20-digit prime numbers (numbers that cannot be evenly divided by a number other than themselves or one). If given a date within the last 40,000 years—or the next 40,000—they can state almost instantly the day of the week on which it falls. The twins can also describe, with uncanny accuracy, the minor events of any day in their lives from the time they were four years old. When a *LIFE* magazine reporter asked them on what day in 1960 a big snowstorm occurred, the answer came without hesitation: "On December 11, a Sunday, about two in the afternoon it started. The weather really went on a toot that day."

George and Charles owe the stark contrasts in their intelligence and ability to function to savant syndrome, an extremely rare condition in which a person with a serious mental handicap, such as severe retardation, autism, or schizophrenia, exhibits an astonishing ability or talent, usually in a single, narrowly defined area. Some savants share George's and Charles's phenomenal skills at calendar calculating. Others are able to perform an intricate Bach or Mozart composition on the piano after hearing it only once. Still others can memorize prodigious amounts of information, such as an entire telephone directory. Scientists do not yet fully understand how these strange skills develop in people like George and Charles, although they suspect it is somehow related to a particular type of brain damage that usually occurs before birth.

Savant syndrome is just one example of the mysterious relationship that exists between the brain, the physical organ of thought, and the mind, the mental process by which an individual feels, remembers, wills, and reasons. Damage to the brain, whether congenital or sustained after birth, frequently results in perplexing disorders of the mind. One man who suffered head injuries in an automobile accident, for instance, was no longer able to recognize faces—even his own in the mirror—although he could easily identify simple schematic objects, such as a watch or a key. A woman with a brain tumor acquired what German neurologists called *Witzelsucht,* or "joking disease," a fundamental sense that everything in life is facetious or insignificant. Scientists believe that the

study of such unusual conditions can lead to a better understanding of how the intangible elements of the mind—emotions and personality—are shaped by the physical workings of the brain.

The human brain is a complex mass of billions of nerve cells, or neurons, and a trillion supporting cells, known as neuroglia. Most of these cells can be found in the cerebral cortex, the wrinkled layer of pinkish gray matter that overlies the rest of the brain and that is believed to be the seat of consciousness and intellectual thought. Cells on the surface of the cerebral cortex process information received from the outside world through the body's senses. The data is then passed on to the interior of the cerebral cortex, where it is combined with information from memory and from other areas of the brain to create consciousness— the feelings, thoughts, images, and ideas that make up an individual's internal psychological world.

Scientists know that the transmission of information within the brain is accomplished by the neurons through electrical impulses. But just how these electrical patterns become the thoughts and sensations of the conscious mind remains a great and profound mystery. Nor do scientists fully understand the workings of the unconscious mind, those basic, instinctual emotions that seem to originate from deep within the brain's oldest and most primitive regions. Recent brain research has revealed that human beings have not one brain, but three. Differing from one another in structure and function, yet intimate-

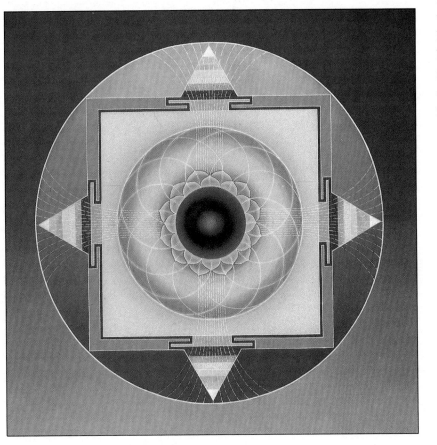

A 1923 phrenology chart links skull areas to attributes of character and intelligence. In the nineteenth century, even some scientists endorsed this system of reading bumps on the head.

brain, which humans inherited from their reptilian forebears. Here are housed the instincts for hunting, fighting, migrating, mating, and establishing territorial control. Surrounding the R-complex is a second mass known as the limbic system, or old mammalian brain. Found in much the same form in all other mammals, the human limbic system is a collection of interconnected structures that help regulate emotion, memory, and certain aspects of movement.

The third mass is the cerebral cortex, sometimes called the new mammalian brain because it has evolved during the past two million years or so, much more recently than the R-complex or limbic system. More highly developed in humans than in any other mammal, the cerebral cortex provides many of the traits that are thought to distinguish humans from other species, such as the abilities to reason, think abstractly, form symbols, and create language and culture.

The development of the cerebral cortex was one of the most significant turning points in the history of biology. "It is this new development that makes possible the insight required to plan for the needs of others as well as the self," observed Paul D. MacLean, a physician and pioneer in brain-structure research at the National Institutes of Mental Health in Poolesville, Maryland. "In creating for the first time a creature with a concern for other living things, nature accomplished a 180-degree turnabout from what had previously been a reptile-eat-reptile and dog-eat-dog world."

The discovery that the human brain has different regions with different functions has led to several structural explanations for the difference between the conscious and unconscious mind. British psychologist Stan Gooch offers

ly interrelated, these three neural masses are believed to have become superimposed one on another during millions of years of evolution. The first, smallest, and most primitive of these masses is known as the R-complex, or reptilian

one such explanation in his 1972 book, *Total Man.* A human is a dual being, Gooch argues, consisting of a rational Ego—the part of the being that is considered the real self—and a darker, more intuitive, and less acknowledged Self. Gooch believes that the Ego is housed in the cerebral cortex, the more modern part of the brain; the Self inhabits a section of the older limbic system known as the cerebellum. The cerebellum regulates and coordinates muscular activity, and according to Gooch, it is also the seat of the unconscious. From that area of the brain, he says, come hypnagogic hallucinations—those frightening, dreamlike images that we occasionally experience in the state between waking and sleeping—and such sinister figures as vampires, troglodytes, and the devil.

Gooch also believes paranormal experiences arise from the cerebellum. In his 1978 book, *The Paranormal,* he describes how, at the age of twenty-six, he experienced a "mediumistic trance." Gooch had accompanied a friend to a séance in Coventry. Soon after the séance began, Gooch felt inexplicably lightheaded. "And then suddenly it seemed to me that a great wind was rushing through the room," he wrote. "In my ears was the deafening sound of roaring waters. . . . As I felt myself swept away I became unconscious." Later, when he again became aware of his surroundings, Gooch was told that several spirits had spoken through him. Gooch understood at once what had happened; he felt, he later wrote, as if he had been possessed. It was a physical sensation, he added, as if the spirits had slipped on his body much as they would a suit of clothes.

In Gooch's opinion, the source of such mystical experiences resides deep within the older reaches of the brain. Other researchers contend, however, that the source of paranormal occurrences lies much closer to the brain's surface—in the right hemisphere of the cerebral cortex. Scientists now know that the two halves of the cerebral cortex, though mirror images of each other, serve very different functions. The left hemisphere, or left brain, controls the right half of the body in most people and is more adept

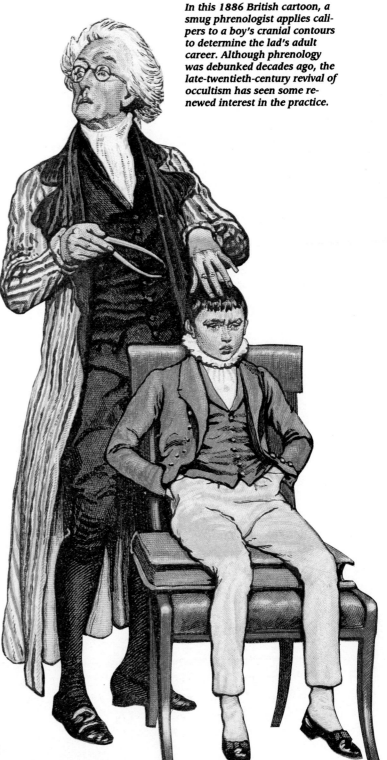

In this 1886 British cartoon, a smug phrenologist applies calipers to a boy's cranial contours to determine the lad's adult career. Although phrenology was debunked decades ago, the late-twentieth-century revival of occultism has seen some renewed interest in the practice.

Return to Eden: The Chimpanzees Speak

According to first-century Jewish historian Josephus, the animals in the Garden of Eden spoke freely with Adam and Eve. But after the sundering of paradise, mutual understanding between beast and human ceased. In recent decades, however, in several primate research laboratories across the United States, the lines of communication seem to have been reopened: Researchers say more than a dozen chimpanzees have learned to speak.

For eons, people believed that language was a unique product of the human mind, a sign of the special relationship between humankind and the Divine. When scientists began to question this assumption, they turned to the chimpanzee, the human species' closest kin in the animal kingdom.

Anatomical differences from humans prevent chimps from speaking aloud. Therefore, researchers chose visual modes of expression for their experiments. In 1966, University of Nevada psychologists adopted a chimp named Washoe. They taught her more than 130 words in American Sign Language (ASL), the silent parlance of the deaf.

The scientists say Washoe created new expressions with words from her vocabulary and also spoke to herself in ASL: "We have often seen Washoe moving stealthily to a forbidden part of the yard signing 'quiet' to herself, or running pell-mell for the potty chair signing 'hurry,' " they reported.

Other chimp language experiments flourished as well. Yet Herb Terrace, a Columbia University psychologist, was not convinced. He maintained that a chimp was not speaking unless it created unique sentences spontaneously, a feat he thought had not been demonstrated by scientific method.

After running his own experiment with a chimpanzee named Nim, to whom Terrace taught more than 200 ASL words, the psychologist decided that the chimp never created his own sentences but rather mimicked his teachers' cues—and that the chimps in all the experiments had mindlessly imitated their keepers. Other researchers disagreed, challenging Terrace with new evidence: Without any help from human beings whatsoever, Washoe taught more than fifty words in ASL to a young male chimp she adopted.

Although even the most articulate chimp used just 200 words—a fraction of a normal human's vocabulary—and communicated only simple ideas, the animals' "achievement is staggering," wrote a science editor in 1979. "Twenty years ago we thought all they could do was hoot." Their feats have defied the notion that the human mind is the sole domain of language.

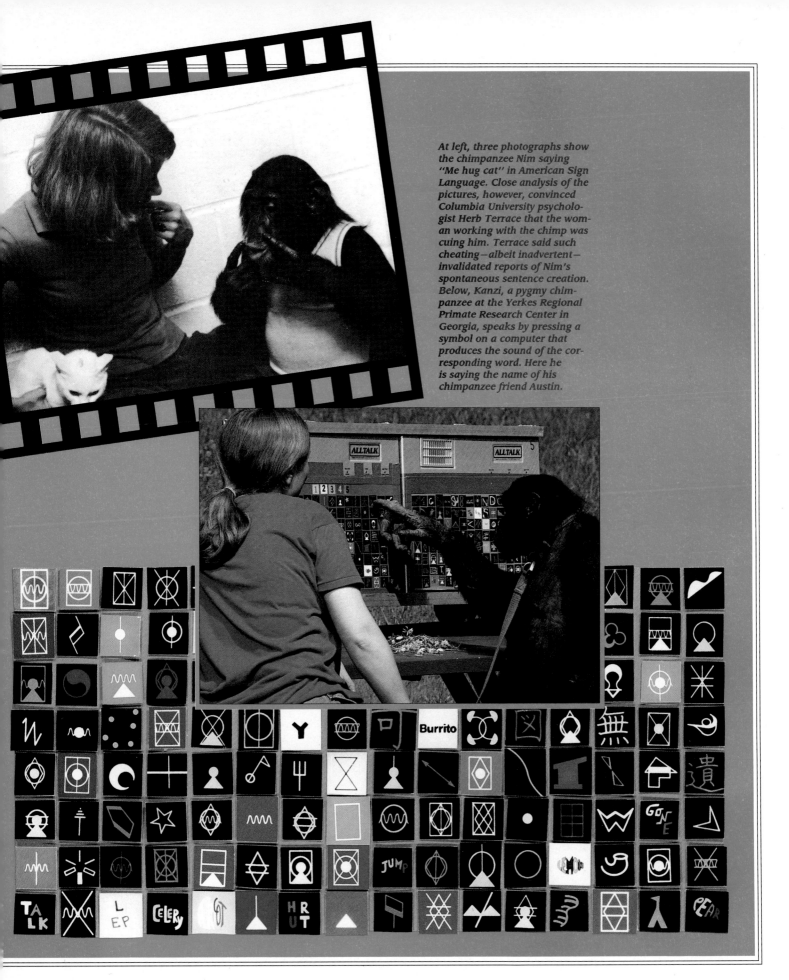

At left, three photographs show the chimpanzee Nim saying "Me hug cat" in American Sign Language. Close analysis of the pictures, however, convinced Columbia University psychologist Herb Terrace that the woman working with the chimp was cuing him. Terrace said such cheating—albeit inadvertent—invalidated reports of Nim's spontaneous sentence creation. Below, Kanzi, a pygmy chimpanzee at the Yerkes Regional Primate Research Center in Georgia, speaks by pressing a symbol on a computer that produces the sound of the corresponding word. Here he is saying the name of his chimpanzee friend Austin.

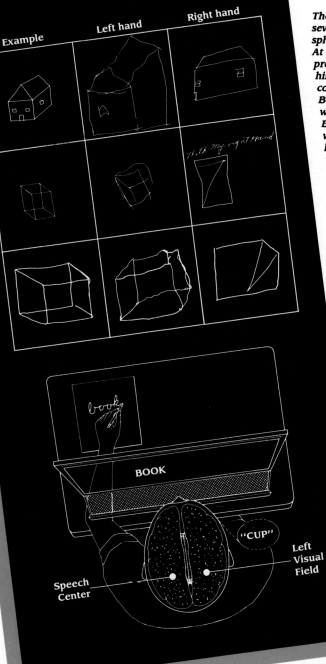

at verbal reasoning, logical thinking, and deciphering abstract symbols such as numbers and words. The right brain controls the left half of the body and is more skilled at nonverbal, intuitive thought. And whereas the left hemisphere processes information in small, analytical steps, the right hemisphere looks at an entire situation all at once and responds accordingly. The right brain, therefore, is believed by many to be the source of both creativity and a certain cosmic wisdom—a higher and more intuitive form of knowledge and understanding.

One researcher who subscribes to that line of thinking is Julian Jaynes, a professor of psychology at Princeton University. Curiosity about why speech areas could be found in only one hemisphere of the human brain led Jaynes to develop a startling theory about human consciousness and mystical experiences. In his controversial 1976 book, *The Origins of Consciousness in the Breakdown of the Bicameral Mind,* Jaynes argued that as recently as 2000 BC, humans possessed no self-awareness, or inner life. As evidence, Jaynes pointed to the Greek poet Homer's *Iliad,* whose characters, he said, were incapable of self-reflection. "The characters of the *Iliad* do not sit down

and think out what to do. They have no conscious minds such as we say we have, and certainly no introspections," wrote Jaynes. Without self-awareness, he added, the characters also have no notion of free will, nor any sense of responsibility for their actions. Instead, it is the gods who intervene in their lives and make them do things. For example, when Achilles accuses Agamemnon of stealing his mistress, Agamemnon claims that the gods made him do it: "Not I was the cause, but Zeus and Destiny and Erinys that walketh in the darkness, who put into my soul fierce madness. . . . What could I do?"

From this observation, Jaynes developed the most controversial element of his theory: In the absence of self-consciousness, the godlike voices that the Greeks of the *Iliad* and other ancient humans heard and responded to were auditory hallucinations. Such hallucinations, Jaynes maintained, are still experienced by modern humans, but usually only during times of stress. Jaynes claims to have experienced a vivid auditory hallucination of his own. It occurred during his late twenties, at a time when he was living alone in Boston and struggling to work out the ideas that later became his theory of the bicameral—or divided—mind. "One afternoon," he wrote, "I lay down in intellectual despair on a couch. Suddenly, out of an absolute quiet, there came a firm, distinct loud voice from my upper right which said, 'Include the knower in the known!' It lugged me to my feet absurdly exclaiming, 'Hello?' looking for whoever was in the room. The voice had an exact location. No one was there!"

Jaynes believes these internal voices originate in the right hemisphere of the brain. "The language of men was involved with only one hemisphere in order to leave the other free for the language of gods," he deduced. Some of the vestiges of "godlike" ability still remain in the right hemisphere of the brain, according to Jaynes, and are expressed in such varied forms as artistic creativity, religious frenzy, and schizophrenia.

Although Hippocrates wrote of the possibility of the duality of the human brain as long ago as 400 BC, for many centuries the idea was largely ignored. The prevalent view was that the brain was a single, integrated organ. One scientist who thought differently was English physician Sir Thomas Browne, who, in 1684, after years of medical observation, proposed that the two hemispheres of the brain might control different types of behavior. In 1745, another physician reported the case of a male patient whose left brain had been badly damaged by a stroke. Because the only word the man spoke was "yes," he was forced to communicate by making signs with his hands. Yet despite this handicap, the report continued, the man could "sing certain hymns, which he had learned before he became ill, as clearly and distinctly as any healthy person." This phenomenon—the ability to sing but not to speak—has since been observed in many brain-damaged patients and is now recognized as one indication that singing and other musical abilities are a right-brain function.

By the mid-nineteenth century, reports of strange behaviors observed in other brain-damaged patients had convinced a small but growing number of scientists that the two brain halves had distinct, specialized functions. The evidence became compelling in April 1861 when French surgeon and neuroanatomist Pierre-Paul Broca made a startling presentation at a meeting of the Paris Anthropological Society. Broca told the story of a patient who, until the time of his death, had suffered from a severe difficulty in speaking known as aphasia. Friends had given the man the nick-name Tan Tan because those were the only words he could utter. Yet, although the man's speech had been severely impaired, he had been able to understand what was said to him and to respond with facial expressions and hand gestures. Only his ability to speak had been restricted.

After telling the story of Tan Tan to the scientists gathered at the Paris meeting, Broca then revealed the exhibit he had brought with him. It was Tan Tan's brain. Pointing to a damaged area about the size of a hen's egg within the brain's left hemisphere, Broca proposed to the membership that this damage had been the cause of Tan Tan's speech problem.

It was a powerful presentation, and many scientists who heard it at the meeting or who read about it later became convinced that certain brain functions—in this case, language—did reside in specific areas of the brain. Other evidence soon followed. In 1874, German neurologist Carl Wernicke reported the discovery of a different type of aphasia caused by damage to another area of the brain's left hemisphere. Unlike Tan Tan, patients with what became known as Wernicke's aphasia had no trouble making verbal sounds. On the contrary, they were extremely verbose. Their impairment involved the inability to make their speech comprehensible to others; it simply came out sounding like gibberish.

Knowledge of the independence of the two brain hemispheres advanced dramatically after the development in the 1940s of a radical surgical procedure for severe and incurable epilepsy. The procedure involved severing the corpus callosum, the thick, pencil-shaped band of some 50 million nerve fibers that connects the right and left hemispheres of the brain and makes possible the transference of information from one hemisphere to the other. Before the development of this daring new surgical procedure, those epileptic patients with incurable seizures that did not respond to medication died from the extensive brain damage caused when the seizure crossed from one brain hemisphere to the other. Surgeons found that by cutting the cor-

P.B. inv.   H. Sculp. Cum priv.

pus callosum, they could restrict seizures to a single hemisphere, thus limiting the resultant damage to brain cells.

Not only was the surgery successful in treating that form of epilepsy, but much to the astonishment and relief of surgeons and patients alike, it also appeared to produce no noticeable change in personality, temperament, or intellectual abilities. One of these so-called split-brain patients, a twelve-year-old boy, was able upon awakening from the surgery to successfully repeat the tongue twister "Peter Piper picked a peck of pickled peppers." Another patient, a World War II veteran whose seizures had started when bomb shrapnel pierced his brain, claimed after the operation to feel better than he had in years. "In casual conversation over a cup of coffee and a cigarette, one would hardly suspect that there was anything at all unusual about him," remarked a neurosurgeon who interviewed the veteran after his surgery.

But subtle neurological changes had occurred, changes that became fully apparent only some twenty years later, when split-brain patients were given a more extensive battery of evaluative tests. Those specially designed tests were conducted at the California Institute of Technology under the guidance of psychobiologist Roger Sperry, who later won a Nobel Prize in physiology and medicine for his split-brain research. The procedures provided startling evidence that the operation had isolated the distinct functions of the brain's two hemispheres.

Sperry and one of his students, Michael Gazzaniga, began their tests on a forty-eight-year-old man nicknamed W. J., who had undergone a split-brain operation to cure his epilepsy. The scientists found that when a simple written instruction, such as "move your hand," was flashed to W. J.'s left visual field—which projects only to the right hemisphere of the brain—W. J. would not respond. Although his right brain had received the message, it could not comprehend its meaning and therefore could not instruct the hand to move. In another experiment, W. J. was given a standard set of red and white blocks to arrange in a picture design. His right hand—controlled by the left side of the brain—was unable to perform the task, but his left hand could do it quite easily. "The claim that we based on those findings," Gazzaniga later recalled, "was that the left hemisphere is dominant for language processes and the right hemisphere is dominant for visual-constructional tasks."

Through the study of W. J. and other split-brain patients, Sperry and Gazzaniga confirmed the remarkable independence of the two brain halves. The hemispheres were even found capable of working simultaneously on different tasks. Using a split-screen monitor, the doctors flashed the word *clap* to a patient's right brain and the word *laugh* to her left brain. She immediately laughed and clapped. But when asked, the woman said the only command she had seen on the screen was the one to laugh. Her right brain could not verbalize the command it had seen—to clap—but could carry it out, even at the same time the left brain was obeying its command to laugh.

This kind of results have led to speculation that within each individual there may exist two separate selves, or personalities, one residing in the brain's left hemisphere, the other in the right. In fact, Gazzaniga has concluded that each hemisphere has its own memories, values, and emotions. At times, he says, they may not agree with each other. For example, when Gazzaniga asked the right hemisphere of a young split-brain patient called Paul what he wanted to be, the answer came back "an automobile racer." But when he asked the same question of Paul's left hemisphere, the answer was "a draftsman." Paul was also periodically given a multiple-choice test in which he was asked to rate some of his interests on a one-to-five scale, from "like very much" to "dislike very much." The test was administered separately to his right and left brains. One day, the answers from the two brains were diametrically opposite each other. Whatever one hemisphere liked, the other disliked. Paul himself was in a very bad temper that day, verbally abusive and argumentative. A month later, on a day when he exhibited a calm and pleasant mood, he took the test again. This time his two hemispheres rated all the items on the test the

Aided by attendants, two women suffering from epilepsy stumble to a healing site in this 1642 engraving. When the group reaches a certain bridge, the men will force their charges to dance to bagpipe music, an exercise that was once believed to purge epileptics of seizures.

Mental Workouts That May Be Worthless—or Worse

"I spend way too much time on my triceps and not enough on my concepts," confessed a client at the Visconti 2000 Mind/Brain Fitness Center in Cambridge, Massachusetts. Like hundreds of others, he resolved to start toning his mind on trendy equipment such as the Synchro-Energizer *(below, right)*.

This brainier cousin of weightlifting machines is a futuristic-looking headpiece with goggles that flash colored lights and headphones that pulse musical tones. Benefits of its audiovisual bombardment reportedly include a balancing of the two hemispheres of the brain that enthusiasts say can relieve stress, end problems with substance abuse, and boost creativity, self-esteem, and even IQ.

The Synchro-Energizer is but one of many such machines. Another, the Lumitron, operates on theories about the psychological effects of color. Mind trainers program its TV screen—mounted inside a canvas hood worn over the head—to display any color of the spectrum deemed appropriate for the client. Red, for instance, allegedly stimulates the brain, while violet is thought to relax it.

The Graham Potentializer—a bed that rotates in a magnetic field to the sound of relaxing music—supposedly soothes an anxiety-ridden client by rocking the fluids of the inner ear. The motion is said to prepare the mind not only for visualization of the accomplishment of goals but even for so-called out-of-body experiences.

Critics note that no controlled experiments have proved the efficacy of any of these machines, which some call the snake oil of the electronic era. In fact, a flashing light such as that projected by the Synchro-Energizer can be dangerous: It may induce epileptic seizures in people susceptible to them.

same. Gazzaniga concluded that the human brain is constantly involved in this type of warring and that dissonance between the two hemispheres may be a very simple cause of anxiety and tension.

Paul's was an extremely unusual case. Whereas the right hemisphere of most split-brain patients is completely mute, his became capable of some language communication. Yet his left hemisphere always remained the dominant of the two and would sometimes use its much superior language skills to rationalize the

Two Italians match wits over a chess game as friends look on in this 1493 woodcut. Thought to have originated in seventh-century India, chess has long been touted as a mind-sharpening exercise.

puzzling actions performed by the right hemisphere. In one test, a picture of a chicken's claw was shown to Paul's left brain while a picture of a snow scene was shown simultaneously to his right. Then he was asked to look at a series of other pictures and choose a shot that corresponded to the one he had just seen. With his right hand, Paul chose a picture of a chicken, and with his left hand he selected a picture of a snow shovel. Paul explained his choices by remarking, "The chicken claw goes with the chicken, and you need a shovel to clean out the chicken's shed." This, of course, was Paul's left hemisphere talking. His right hemisphere could not speak for itself and explain why it had chosen the snow shovel, so his left hemisphere, which had no knowledge of the snow-scene picture, constructed as plausible an explanation as it could.

The behavioral anomalies of people who have undergone split-brain surgery are usually quite different from those who have experienced damage through injury or dis-

ease to a specific area of either the right or left hemisphere. For example, few split-brain patients experience trouble speaking after their surgery, for although the left brain has been severed from the right, it has not experienced any direct damage. But, as Paul Broca and Carl Wernicke discovered more than a century ago, direct damage to one of the main speech centers in the left hemisphere will leave an individual either unable to speak or unable to produce meaningful speech. Damage to other areas of the left brain can cause

such specific disorders as name amnesia, an inability to recall names of familiar people, or word deafness, a condition in which a person can read, write, and speak normally but is unable to comprehend spoken words.

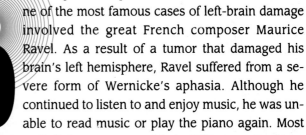

ne of the most famous cases of left-brain damage involved the great French composer Maurice Ravel. As a result of a tumor that damaged his brain's left hemisphere, Ravel suffered from a severe form of Wernicke's aphasia. Although he continued to listen to and enjoy music, he was unable to read music or play the piano again. Most frustrating of all, however, was his inability to write down the cascade of musical notes he heard in his head. From 1926 until his death, at age sixty-two, following a 1937 brain operation, Ravel never composed again.

Injuries to the right hemisphere of the brain disrupt visual perception and spatial orientation rather than language skills. Many right-brain-damaged people, for example, have difficulty putting together simple jigsaw puzzles or following directions on a map. They also become disoriented easily and may wander about lost in familiar places, including their own homes. Musicians whose right brains are injured often forget how to play their instruments or how to sing, a condition known as amusia.

Perhaps one of the most bizarre, and rare, conditions caused by damage to the brain's right hemisphere is neglect syndrome, a neurological disorder that leaves people behaving as if the left side

Besides discovering a speech center in the brain, Pierre-Paul Broca also investigated the limbic region, which is now known to be linked to emotion.

of their visual perception—and even the left side of their bodies—no longer exists. A man with this disorder may shave only the right side of his face, or a woman may apply lipstick to only the right half of her lips. When asked to copy a picture of a house or a clock, people with neglect syndrome draw only the right-hand side of the object—and think nothing is amiss. Sometimes, such patients can have a complete loss of awareness of their left arms or legs and in extreme cases may not even acknowledge that the limbs belong to them. Oliver Sacks wrote of one such man whom he encountered lying on the floor in a hospital ward. The man claimed that someone had tried to play a horrific joke on him by attaching a severed leg to his body. No matter how hard he tried, said the frightened man, he could not tear the disgusting limb from his flesh. Sacks calmed the patient, gently explaining that the leg belonged to the man and not to a cadaver. The patient was not easily convinced, however. Sacks then asked him where he thought his left leg was, if the leg he was trying to remove was not it. "I don't know," said the man. "I have no idea. It's disappeared. It's gone. It's nowhere to be found."

Other damage to the brain specifically affects the

senses—the ability to see, touch, hear, smell, or feel. In a condition known as agnosia, which means "absence of recognition," a person can identify the properties of an object, but not the object itself. Usually, the impairment involves just one sense, depending on where in the brain the damage has occurred. Visual agnosia, or mind blindness, can be particularly disabling. The mind fails to see the whole of a scene or object and instead takes in only details. When looking at a photograph, for example, a patient with visual agnosia may be able to recognize an automobile or a building or a person walking but will not be able to put these elements together to recognize that it is a photograph of a city street. To identify what they cannot recognize by sight alone, people with visual agnosia must use their other senses. When one man with very severe visual agnosia was shown a rose, he could not identify it at all. When he was permitted to touch it, he described it abstractly as "a convoluted red form with a linear green attachment." Only when he was told to smell the flower did he guess its true identity.

The specific inability to recognize faces, even one's own, is known as prosopagnosia. This form of agnosia seems to arise from damage to the right side of the occipital lobe, the visual center of the brain located at the rear of the cerebral cortex. Because the area of the brain responsible for voice recognition is on the opposite side of the brain, a person with prosopagnosia usually can place the faces of friends and relatives as soon as they start to speak. In some instances, patients lose not only the ability to recognize faces but the very idea of a "face."

Damage to the brain can cause even broader concepts

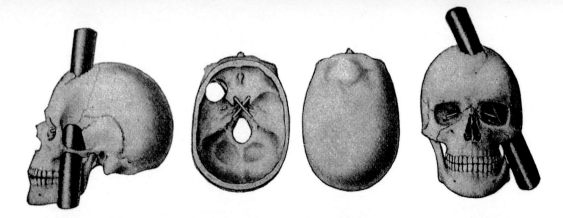

to be lost to the mind. In one highly unusual case reported by Oliver Sacks, a stroke patient suffered such extensive damage to the occipital lobe that he became completely blind—but did not know it. "He had lost all visual images and memories, lost them totally—yet had no sense of any loss," wrote Sacks. "Indeed, he had lost the very idea of seeing—and was not only unable to describe anything visually, but was bewildered when I used words such as 'seeing' and 'light.' He

Drawings re-create the dramatic head injury sustained in 1848 by Phineas Gage. Remarkably, he recovered fully, or so it seemed until his friends recognized that he was "no longer Gage." From this incident, scientists learned that damage to the frontal cortex affects personality.

Author of the book that inspired the 1990 film Awakenings, New York neurologist Oliver Sacks exudes a sober compassion in this photograph. His chronicles brought the mysterious world of brain disorders to public attention.

had become, in essence, a nonvisual being."

In rare and tragic cases involving neurological damage, people lose a form of sensation scientists have named proprioception, which is the awareness of the physical body. From the Latin meaning "received from self," proprioception is the hidden sense that enables the mind to be aware of the location and movement of the body's muscles and limbs. It works with great precision and with very little conscious effort. The decision to clap one's hands, for example, takes a moment of conscious thought, but once the decision has been made, the body carries forth the order without much self-awareness. It can even be done with the eyes shut—all because of proprioception.

For a person who has lost this sense, clapping two hands together takes extreme concentration and effort. Without a sense of where the body is in space, putting two hands together becomes an almost impossible task. The person is not paralyzed—the muscles are still capable of movement—but *disembodied*. Patients without proprioception feel as if they have "lost" their arms or legs. "I think they're one place, and I find they're another," noted one woman who developed the condition at age twenty-seven. "It's like the body's blind."

The woman eventually learned to move again by using her vision to compensate for the loss of proprioception. She spent hour after hour monitoring her movements, watching each part of her body carefully as it moved. She learned how to stand erect, walk, hold a knife and fork, even type at a computer—in short, to do all the simple, unpremeditated movements of everyday life. Yet for her, such movements were no longer natural and effortless but required an immense and conscious effort. Everything had to be done by vision, not feel. If she let her concentration slip for even a second, she would collapse onto the floor.

Damage to the brain does not always have a debilitating outcome, however. Occasionally a physiological change will occur in the brain that enhances the senses or that unleashes a hidden sensory potential of which most humans are not normally aware. Indeed, some scientists believe that many phenomena often attributed to a sixth sense—such as telepathy and clairvoyance—are really the result of one or more of the five standard senses going haywire and functioning in a supernormal way. For example, in the rare brain disorder called synesthesia, discovered more than two centuries ago, the senses are joined in a mysterious way that enables people to actually see sounds, feel flavors, and taste colors or words. To a synesthete, the sound of a telephone ringing may look like diamond-shaped blocks, or the word *telephone* may taste like apple pie. The most common form of synesthesia is called *audition colorée,* or "colored hearing." "One of the things I love about my husband," noted one synesthete, "are the colors of his voice and his laugh. It's a wonderful golden brown, with a flavor of crisp, buttery toast, which sounds very odd, I know, but it is very real."

Intrigued by such perplexing comments, Washington, D.C., neurologist Richard Cytowic monitored the brains of synesthetic people as they were actually experiencing colored sounds and discovered an unusual pattern of blood flow. Normally, blood flow increases in the cerebral cortex during sensory stimulation. Cytowic found, however, that when a person is "seeing" sounds, blood flow decreases in the cerebral cortex and increases in the deeper and more primitive limbic system. "The brain's higher information processing turns off during colored hearing," Cytowic said. "An older, more fundamental way of viewing the world—more mammalian than language-related—takes over." According to Cytowic and other researchers who have studied the phenomenon, many ordinary people continue to exhibit rudimentary remnants of synesthesia. For example, they experience lower and higher musical tones as having different colorations and see the various days of the week as having different colors.

A variation of synesthesia is the condition known as "skin vision," or eyeless sight. Although this strange phenomenon was first reported in the 1920s by the French novelist and physician Jules Romains, scientists did not begin to take it seriously until 1962—when a young Russian woman named Rosa Kuleshova first astonished members of Moscow's Biophysics Institute of the Soviet Academy of Sciences by her apparent ability to read printed words and distinguish colors with her fingers. Kuleshova told the scientists that the ability had developed gradually, beginning with the third and fourth fingers of her right hand, then spreading to all her fingers, eventually reaching her elbow and other body parts as well.

When the news of Kuleshova's seemingly psychic ability was made public, she became an overnight sensation. The young woman was invited to demonstrate her talents on stage. She was overwhelmed by the sudden attention, however, and soon began making extravagant claims that she could fulfill only by cheating. Despite her transgressions, researchers of the phenomenon believed Kuleshova's abilities were genuine and with further investigation discovered that they were not unique. A Soviet professor named Abram Novomeysky reported that of the persons he tested, one in six of those could learn within half an hour to differentiate between two colors by touch. Like Kuleshova, some subjects eventually learned to identify all primary colors by their feel. Most of those tested agreed on how the different colors "felt." They said that yellow, for example, was slippery, and that orange was hard and rough. Some subjects honed their skills to such a degree that they no longer needed to touch the colors. They explained that since each hue radiated its particular texture to a different height, it was possible to identify a color by merely passing a hand over it. Red appeared to radiate highest and light blue lowest. From this research, Novomeysky came to believe that skin vision was the result of an interaction between electromagnetic fields emanating both from the "reader's" fingertips and from the color being read.

Just as some people display remarkable sensory abilities, such as skin vision or colored hearing, others have an extraordinary capacity for memory. The nineteenth-century English historian Thomas Macaulay was said to have such a remarkable memory that he could quote a chapter of a book verbatim after reading it only once. To win a wager, he once memorized John Milton's epic *Paradise Lost* in a single night. Also credited with incredible mnemonic powers was the Yugoslav-born American inventor Nikola Tesla. He never wrote mathematical problems down on paper but instead worked them out entirely in his head. Tesla was also able to "see" his inventions in his mind long before he sketched blueprints for them. These mental images were so precise and detailed that they included dimensions down to ten-thousandths of an inch.

The design for a new machine sometimes popped into Tesla's mind quite unexpectedly. Such was the case with his most famous invention, the alternating-current generator, a device that ushered in the age of electricity. One evening in 1882, while walking with a companion in a park in Prague, Tesla apparently fell into a sudden trancelike state. His body swayed slowly from side to side; his arms flailed the air. Then he saw it: a clear and detailed vision of an alternating-current motor, a machine unknown at that time. "The idea came like a flash of lightning, and in an instant the truth was revealed," Tesla recalled later. "The images I saw were wonderfully sharp and clear and had the solidity of metal and stone, so much so that I told him [the friend], 'See my motor here; watch me reverse it.' I cannot describe my emotions. Pygmalion seeing his statue come to life could not have been more deeply moved." Despite his excitement, Tesla did not rush back to his laboratory to make a rough sketch of his new invention. He knew the machine's image would remain etched in his memory indefinitely. Indeed, a year later, when Tesla was finally ready to make a working model of the generator, the image was as sharp and clear in his mind as it had been the day he had first envisioned it.

Both Macaulay and Tesla had eidetic, or photographic, memory, the ability to summon up visual images with ex-

traordinary accuracy. Many young children possess this type of memory, as evidenced by their ability to describe drawings from their favorite storybooks in minute detail. For reasons that remain unknown, however, the power is rarely retained past puberty. Some scientists believe that the brain becomes more selective as it matures; rather than remembering an entire drawing from a book, the adult brain remembers only the most relevant images and then tosses out the rest.

Eidetic memory appears to be literally limitless. As reported in the 1990 edition of the *Guinness Book of World Records,* in 1967, one Mehmed Ali Halici of Turkey recited from memory 6,666 verses of the Koran in six hours. And in 1989, Englishman Tony Power memorized in correct order a random sequence of thirteen packs of shuffled playing cards—676 cards in all—after looking at them only once. But the world record for a single eidetic memory feat may be held by Bhandanta Vicitasara of Rangoon, Burma, who in 1974 correctly recited from memory 16,000 pages of Buddhist canonical texts.

These feats notwithstanding, the most celebrated case of a mnemonist, or "person with a vast and endless memory," is that of a man known simply as S., a patient of the great Soviet psychologist Aleksandr Luria. In the early 1920s, the young S., a reporter for a Moscow paper, went to see Luria at the suggestion of his editor. The editor had been astounded by S.'s memory skills—at his ability, for example, to remember long lists of addresses and detailed assignment instructions without taking notes. Luria, who had always been fascinated by memory and its capabilities, immediately tested S. by asking him to repeat several random series of words and numbers. The reporter complied with ease. Luria increased the number of elements in the series from thirty to fifty, and then to seventy. He presented them to S. in writing as well as orally. But the reporter's performance remained steadfast; he never made an error.

"As the experimenter, I soon found myself in a state verging on utter confusion," Luria wrote of this first meeting with S. "An increase in the length of a series led to no

The Senses: Bringing the World Inside

Gateways to consciousness, the senses gather information from external reality and relay it to the brain. They supply the mind with food for thought, and all awareness depends upon their input.

Most human beings possess smell, touch, taste, hearing, and vision, but people lacking one or more of these compensate by sharpening their remaining senses or even by developing new ones. The blind, for instance, often maneuver by a kind of sonar system resembling that of such dwellers in darkness as bats, pit vipers, and whales. They discriminate among objects by reading their different echoes.

Helen Keller, both blind and deaf, cultivated intense awareness of smell, touch, and taste. She could discern people's professions simply by their odor, and she distinguished cornets from strings in a symphony broadcast over the radio by feeling the vibrations from the box with her hands.

Scientists have learned that consciousness receives only a fraction of the data collected by the senses because a filtering system protects the mind from sensory overload. Yet this mechanism also limits perception of reality. An Australian physicist likens this restricted world-view to being "a prisoner in a tower permitted to look through five slits at the landscape outside." These slits widen, however, for those under the influence of drugs or in the throes of disease. People suffering from an adrenal disorder called Addison's disease, for example, are 150 times more sensitive to taste than are healthy people.

Some people, such as successful dowsers or reputed psychics, supposedly draw upon an unexplained mode of perception—a sixth sense. Researchers have found that many of these apparent miracle workers suffered brain damage earlier in life. The trauma may have disturbed the mind's sensory filter system, purportedly allowing a host of paranormal experiences to enter consciousness.

SMELL

Brains evolved over the eons from olfactory stalks; thus the earliest creatures could smell before they could think. Today the ancient sense of smell wields a subtle power, enhancing survival of the species by facilitating the sexual response that certain scents trigger. For example, girls who live among men—and hence smell them—reach puberty sooner than those who do not. Similarly, a male sexually involved with a woman grows facial hair faster than one who is not, because the female odor encourages the production of testosterone.

TOUCH

Experiencing touch is vital to development. In a study on premature infants in hospital incubators, an experimental group was physically stimulated through gentle massage while a control group was not. The massaged babies gained weight 47 percent faster than those who were not touched. Furthermore, their nervous systems matured faster and they were discharged from the hospital an average of six days earlier. Experiments with baby monkeys show that those who experience even slight deprivation of touch suffer actual brain damage.

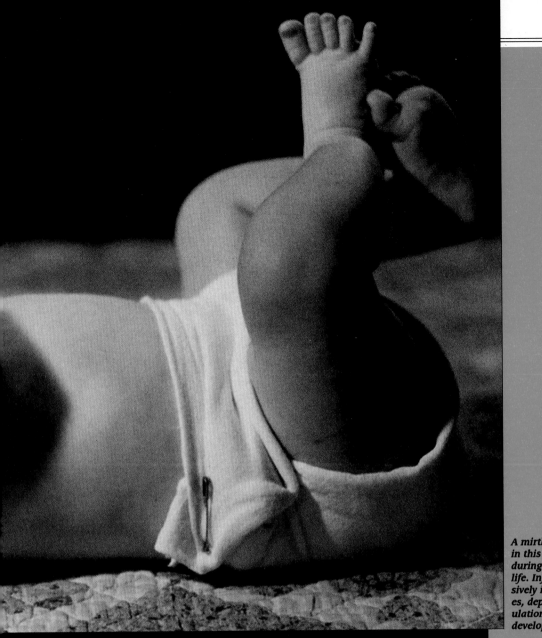

A mirthful baby clasps its hands in this photograph snapped during the first few months of life. Infants dwell almost exclusively in the realm of the senses, dependent upon ample stimulation of all five for timely development and good health.

TASTE

At the start of French novelist Marcel Proust's largely autobiographical book *Swann's Way,* the main character mingles in his mouth a sip of tea and a few morsels of a small shell-shaped cake called a madeleine. So evocative is the sense of taste that this simple act recalls for him an entire era of his childhood. Ten thousand buds dotting the inside of the mouth equip humans with the ability to taste substances sweet, salty, sour, and bitter. All other flavors are actually odors: An air shaft connecting the mouth and nose links the olfactory and gustatory senses.

HEARING

The ability to hear inspires in human beings a panoply of emotions, ranging from the fury induced by the throbbing drums in a macumba ritual to the reflective calm evoked by repeating the Indian mantra ''om.'' From the moment of conception, a fetus grows in comfort hearing the reassuring regularity of its mother's heartbeat. Doctors use music to stimulate comatose patients and to draw out autistic children. And when human beings hear their own voices raised in song, their levels of endorphins—feel-good chemicals in the brain—rise.

SIGHT

A tireless seeker of beauty, the eye has guided much of cultural development since humans first walked the earth. In order to meet the sight organ's rigorous standards, people have long sought to make the world—and themselves—more lovely to behold. Women of Renaissance Italy and Victorian England, for instance, dropped the juice of the poisonous belladonna plant into their eyes to dilate their pupils. And some modern men and women endure endless exercise workouts and even undergo surgery in the quest for an eye-pleasing body.

noticeable increase in difficulty for S., and I simply had to admit that the capacity of his memory had no distinct limits; that I had been unable to perform what one would think was the simplest task a psychologist can do: measure the capacity of an individual's memory."

Intrigued, Luria asked S. to return for more tests. Thus began a professional relationship that would last for thirty years. In 1968, Luria published the results of his experiments with the Moscow reporter in a now classic book, *The Mind of a Mnemonist.*

Luria learned that S. not only had far better recall than most people but that he also underwent the process of memorizing in a unique way. Because he could see clearly in his mind the numbers or words he memorized, S. merely called up the sequence he wanted and then read it back. It made little difference whether he was asked to "read" the sequence from beginning to end or end to beginning, or to skip about in some fashion and recite, say, every third item.

As Luria discovered, when S. reeled off a sequence of words or numbers, he was seeing in his mind not the actual symbols that create the words or numbers but distinctive forms. S.'s memory was based on synesthesia; he saw colored splotches, lines, and other patterns when he heard sounds or when he looked at numbers. "For me 2, 4, 6, 5 are not just numbers," S. wrote in his journal. "They have forms." The number 2, he said, is flat and rectangular and tinted a whitish gray; the number 5 is "absolutely complete and takes the form of a cone or a tower—something substantial." Just as educators have discovered in recent years that children learn best when all their senses are involved, so Luria found that S.'s synesthetic skills enhanced his memorization. "I recognize a word not only by the images it evokes but by a whole complex of feelings that image arouses," S. told Luria. "It's hard to express.... It's not a matter of vision or hearing but some overall sense I get. Usually I experience a word taste and weight, and I don't have to make an effort to remember it—the word seems to recall itself. But it's difficult to describe. What I sense is

something oily slipping through my hand ... or I'm aware of a slight tickling in my left hand caused by a mass of tiny, lightweight points. When that happens I simply remember, without having to make the attempt."

Because sounds and words became fused with images, both conversation and reading were difficult for S. "Even when I read about circumstances that are entirely new to me, if there happens to be a description, say, of a staircase, it turns out to be the one in a house I once lived in," he lamented. "I start to follow it and lose the gist of what I am reading." With his mind cluttered with so many erroneous details, S. found it difficult to lead a normal life. Although he married and had a child, his relationship with his family was a distant one, perceived through a haze by a mind burdened with endless images. He tried many different jobs, from stock-market analyst to vaudeville actor, but each seemed to present obstacles with which he could not cope. Eventually he became a professional "memory man," earning his living astounding audiences with his unparalleled feats of recall. Emotionally, it was a difficult, isolated life. As Luria wrote, "An individual whose conscious awareness is such that a sound becomes fused with a sense of color and taste; for whom each fleeting impression engenders a vivid, inextinguishable image; for whom words have quite different meanings than they do for us—such a person cannot mature in the same way others do, nor will his inner world, his life history tend to be like others."

Centuries ago, the ability to memorize prodigious amounts of information was considered an art tinged with magic. Ancient Greeks and Romans believed that calling upon past knowledge was a way of transcending one's immediate surroundings and, thus, of reaching a higher consciousness, a more intense reality. The memorization of great written works was seen as the key to wisdom as well as to knowledge, and as a renewable source of creative inspiration. Indeed, the Greeks made the goddess of memory, Mnemosyne, the mother of the nine Muses.

One of the most ardent practitioners of the art of memory was Giulio Camillo, a sixteenth-century Italian pro-

fessor who spent much of his life designing a "memory theater." Camillo was quite famous in his day, and his theater, though never completed, was considered one of the great wonders of the world. The theater was circular, with a small central stage surrounded by seven tiers. The tiers were divided by aisles to form seven sections, representing Solomon's seven pillars of wisdom and the seven planets then known to astronomers. Each section had numerous exhibits of paintings, statues, or other objects meant to symbolize all of human knowledge. Under the exhibits were drawers containing various speeches based on Cicero, the unsurpassed orator of ancient Rome. Explaining the purpose behind his theater, Camillo observed, "it is right that we, wishing to store up eternally the eternal nature of all things which can be expressed in speech . . . should assign them to eternal places." Visitors were encouraged to spend time at each exhibit, to absorb the wisdom represented there and thus achieve a deeper and more meaningful sense of reality. It was Camillo's hope that the theater would "keep the mind awake and move the memory," enabling each visitor "to perceive with his eyes everything that is otherwise hidden in the depths of the human mind."

Camillo was not the only scholar of his day to believe that memory possessed magical powers. Italian philosopher and cosmologist Giordano Bruno was convinced that the human mind was divine and contained within it the secrets of the heavens. If human beings could only discover this treasure, using the magical art of memory, he wrote in his 1582 book *The Art of Memory,* they would have at their fingertips all the forces of the cosmos.

The magical powers of the memory still elude most people today, including those researchers who are trying to find and map the source of the human memory and understand its capabilities. One of the first scientists to embark on that quest was the American neuropsychologist Karl Lashley. Starting in the 1920s, Lashley conducted a series of experiments on laboratory rats in which he systematically removed different areas of the animals' brains in an attempt

Ancient Tricks for Storing Thoughts

In the premodern world, where paper was scarce and such conveniences as computer disks and tape recorders unheard of, a sound memory was vital to success. Thus, people intent upon leaving their mark toiled diligently to expand their minds' storage bins of information, striving to catch evanescent thoughts before they plummeted into oblivion.

In classical Greece and Rome, memory was so highly valued that it was called an art. The earliest remaining treatise on it, penned by an anonymous first-century-BC Roman, described a complex mnemonic, or memory-assisting, strategy that involved crafting in the mind a warehouse for personal symbols.

The first step in this process, according to the writer, was to visualize a familiar place, preferably a large house or a spacious public building with plentiful

NEGATIO AFFIRMATIO

GRAMATICA·

nooks and crannies. This served as the mental home for ideas to be memorized. The next task was to devise a symbol for each idea—something unusual or jarring enough to stick in the memory. These symbols were then placed in proper order in succeeding rooms in the house. To recall the entire group of thoughts, one visualized walking through the house and converting each symbol into the idea it signified.

Despite the fact that many people considered this method cumbersome and more likely to thwart than nurture memory, several writers echoed the nameless Roman during both the classical period and the Renaissance. In the sixteenth century, a German monk named Johannes Romberch wrote a similar scheme of recall in which the symbols for ideas were linked not to a single edifice but rather to a group, as illustrated at left above. The various buildings of an abbey became repositories for memory-jogging signs. Romberch also used as a mnemonic device a human figure thematically related to the subject to be memorized. In the drawing above, Gramatica, the personification of grammar, stands amid words and symbols intended to trigger recall of grammatical rules.

to pinpoint exactly where among the elaborately interlaced neurons memory is stored. In 1950, Lashley published a paper titled "In Search of the Engram," in which he reluctantly concluded that memory and learning are not centered in any one area of the brain but are instead diffused throughout it.

At the same time Lashley was admitting that memory could not be localized within the brain, another researcher, Canadian neurosurgeon Wilder Penfield, witnessed some strange events that seemed to indicate it could. To find the tiny scarred areas of the brain where epileptic seizures originate, Penfield had devised a procedure in which he could painlessly stimulate specific surface areas of the cerebral cortex with a small electrical probe. Because the patients remained conscious throughout the procedure, they could describe any sensations they experienced.

Quite unexpectedly, Penfield discovered that his probe could stimulate extremely detailed and often quite emotional memories when it touched areas of the temporal cortex, the portion of the cerebral cortex directly connected to the limbic system. The patients seemed to vividly relive the sights, sounds, tastes, and emotions of long-forgotten experiences. "Oh, gosh," exclaimed one twelve-year-old boy. "There they are, my brother is there. He is aiming an air rifle at me." Observed a young woman of her experience with the probe, "I had the same very, very familiar memory, in an office somewhere. I was there and someone was calling to me, a man leaning on the desk with a pencil in his hand." Other patients heard specific pieces of music, which they could hum note for note. One man was transported back to the South African farm where he used to live.

From his research, Penfield concluded that the brain records every sensation, every emotion, every experience of life yet offers only limited access to that immense store of information. Forgetting, therefore, is not the loss of memories but the inability to locate them. Penfield also concluded that the temporal cortex contained at least some of the neurons directly involved with memory. Scientists now believe, however, that although Penfield was placing his probe on the surface of the temporal cortex, it was really the underlying limbic system that the neurosurgeon was stimulating. More recent research has shown that several structures within this ancient part of the brain play a crucial role in memory formation.

One of those structures is the thalamus, a pea-size area at the center of the brain that serves as a relay station for almost all information coming into the brain. Damage to nerve cells within the thalamus has been directly linked to Korsakoff's syndrome, a memory disorder named for the Russian doctor who first described its symptoms in 1887. People with this disorder, which is usually caused by chronic alcoholism, have no recent memory and sometimes experience what is called retrograde amnesia, in which long stretches of memory may be obliterated. Victims of Korsakoff's syndrome can typically recall events in their distant past, but new memories cannot be established, nor can any new information be learned.

In *The Man Who Mistook His Wife for a Hat,* Oliver Sacks wrote about a forty-nine-year-old man he encountered in 1975. Jimmie, an affable ex-navy officer from Connecticut, had lost thirty years of memory to Korsakoff's syndrome. For Jimmie, it was always 1945 and he was perpetually nineteen years old. Anything new said or shown to him was forgotten within a few seconds' time. "He is," Sacks noted, "isolated in a single moment of being, with a moat or lacuna of forgetting all round him. . . . He is a man without a past (or future), stuck in a constantly changing, meaningless moment."

In another tragic case, a man known in medical literature simply by the initials H. M. led neuroscientists to implicate another structure of the limbic system—the hippocampus—in memory formation. One of the most ancient parts of the brain, the hippocampus is an inch-long curved section of gray matter located within the temporal cortex. In 1953, H. M. underwent a specialized form of brain surgery, devised just for him, to relieve the severe and life-threatening epileptic seizures he was experiencing almost daily. The surgeons intended to remove only H. M.'s temporal lobes, but they inadvertently removed part of his hippocampus as well.

Soon after the operation, H. M.'s doctors realized something had gone terribly wrong. Although his seizures had stopped, H. M. was unable to remember the names or even the faces of the nurses caring for him. If he left his room to walk down the hall, he could not remember how to return. When given a magazine, he would read the same article over and over without realizing he had read it before. His memory was fine for events that had happened prior to his operation, but he could not learn anything new. Like patients with Korsakoff's syndrome, H. M. had lost his ability to remember. He was a man forever stuck in the distant past and instantaneous present.

In many ways mentally retarded, but displaying uncanny pockets of genius, bespectacled twins Charles (left) and George ponder a math problem in 1966. Asked how they could remember so much information—300-figure digits, for example—they said, "We see it."

A horseman sketched with professional-looking detail sits astride an excellently proportioned mount in this drawing by a six-year-old autistic girl called Nadia. Far below average in language and social skills, the child created artwork astonishing in its sophistication.

Whereas H. M. had consciousness without memory, people with savant syndrome—such as the twins, George and Charles, who were described earlier—have memory without consciousness. Savants are renowned for their exceptional eidetic memory in their particular island of talent—the twins' ability to describe the weather conditions of any past day in their lives, for example. The memory of savants, however, is automatic and habitual; it shows absolutely no sign of self-reflection, no cognitive awareness, and little emotional involvement.

Nevertheless, savants display quite extraordinary gifts. Alonzo Clemens, who suffered brain injury after a fall at age three, has an estimated IQ of forty. He can barely count to ten, and his vocabulary is limited to several hundred words—similar to that of a two-year-old child. Yet when handed a lump of clay, he can mold it into a magnificently detailed horse, dog, or other animal, with every muscle and tendon of the animal painstakingly revealed. His pieces are collected by art connoisseurs around the world, fetching prices as high as $45,000. Similarly, an autistic sixteen-year-old boy named Steven Wilcher has dazzled all of his native England with his ability to sketch buildings, bridges, cars—just about anything—from memory, with perfect perspective and exact detail, in just a few minutes. Oliver Sacks, who has observed the boy, speculates that Wilcher's autism somehow allows him to hold thousands of complex patterns in his mind simultaneously.

Another savant, Leslie Lemke, has the triple handicap of blindness, mental retardation, and cerebral palsy. Yet he has enthralled audiences around the world with his remarkable piano-playing abilities. He can play a piece of music flawlessly after hearing it only once, whether it is a sonata by Ludwig van Beethoven or a rock song by the Beatles. After listening to a forty-five-minute opera tape a single time, he can transpose the music to the piano and, as he plays, sing the opera's libretto—in the foreign language in which he heard it.

Both artistic and musical genius are common among savants. Many of them also display evidence of extra-sensory perception. In 1978, a San Diego psychologist by the name of Bernard Rimland published a study of the case histories of approximately 5,400 savant children from around the world. He determined that 561 of them, or a little more than 10 percent, exhibited signs of unusual perception. The parents of these special youngsters were usually the first to notice their child's inexplicable clairvoyance. "He seems to be very psychic," reported the parent of a boy savant who generally rode the school bus home. "We would decide to pick up George from school suddenly, if we were in the area. He would tell the teacher we were coming, and he would come to open the door when we arrived. So he has many special abilities, but cannot write his name or write a sentence." The parents of another savant reported how the youngster had "an extraordinary ability to hear conversations out of range of hearing, and to pick up thoughts not spoken."

Just how savants' brains differ from normal brains and enable them to do all they do is not clear. But psychiatrist Darold Treffert, a leading expert on savant syndrome, believes that the syndrome is caused by damage to the brain's left hemisphere, usually incurred before birth. To compensate for this damage, the right hemisphere becomes over-developed, growing larger than normal and assuming dominance of the entire brain. The imbalance can, in extreme cases, result in a savant—an individual whose right-brain skills are highly developed but whose left-brain abilities are only minimal.

Treffert stresses that the significance of savant syndrome "lies in our inability to explain it. The savants stand as a clear reminder of our ignorance about ourselves, especially about how our brains function. For no model of brain function, particularly memory, will be complete until it can include and account for this remarkable condition." Many other scientists concur with Treffert. It is through the study of such rare and enigmatic disorders, they believe, that the mysterious relationship between the three-pound mass of gray matter and the seemingly amorphous mind will someday become clear.

Art from Outsiders Looking In

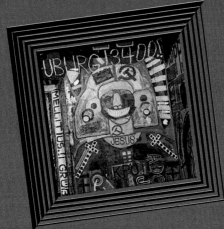

The paintings hang in prestigious galleries around the world, and some artists acknowledge them as masterpieces. Brimming with vivid colors and distorted shapes, sometimes layered with allusive words or phrases, they might be products of an avant-garde movement devoted to raw emotionality. But the artists are not adherents of any school—in fact, their only common trait is mental illness.

Links between madness and creativity have fascinated medical specialists for centuries. Cesare Lombroso, an Italian criminologist and one of the first to advance a theory on the subject, suggested in the late 1800s that genius was a pathological state. He averred that only the absence of reason allowed access to hallucination and illusion, "a true source of artistic and literary inspiration." Later researchers discarded Lombroso's theory and saw the art of the mentally ill as a way to delve into the depths of the artists' unconscious minds. Forms and colors expressed each artist's emotional past, recurring themes changed with age or development of the illness, and a cure might extinguish the creativity altogether.

At one Austrian hospital, this so-called outsider art has spawned a unique experiment—a residence for more than a dozen mentally ill artists and poets. The Haus der Künstler (house of artists) in Gugging encourages and celebrates its residents' work. Widely shown and published, the art illuminates the artists' troubled minds and provides new perspectives on the world, viewed from outside the bounds of cultural—and cognitive—orthodoxy.

Two residents pose before the decorated south front of the Haus der Künstler (above), while three others stand at a second-floor window. The wall paintings are the highly personalized expressions of resident artists. Other styles predominate on the brightly painted east side of the building (right), where some of the artists have proudly signed their work.

Jeshahr checks a navigator's pulse midway through an astral jaunt. Pilot and navigator employ special techniques to synchronize their heartbeats and match their body temperatures as closely as possible before the astral body's departure.

Watching over the astral travelers, Jeshahr operates a panel of "parascientific and electrotechnical" instruments. Said to enhance flying conditions, the controls allegedly adjust the lab's electromagnetic fields.

the human body feels neither hot nor cold. Wearing a special breathing apparatus, Lilly climbed naked into the tank to float in the seemingly gravity-free darkness.

Later versions of the apparatus came to be called sensory-deprivation tanks, but Lilly reported no deprivation. In fact, he found that the absence of external stimulation quickly gave rise to heightened inner awareness; he reported experiencing trances, dreams, mystical visions, and out-of-body travels. He concluded that when sensory input was removed, the brain—which he dubbed a "biocomputer"—released its own program of sensory experiences, limited only by one's imagination.

To Lilly, a trip in the tank was liberating; he could choose programs that took him to various transcendent states of consciousness. "There you are suspended in an embryonic silence," he later wrote, "and suddenly the Logos, the Universal Vibration, begins to pervade the fabric of awareness, coming at once from inside and all directions."

Floating in the waters at NIMH, John Lilly began to wonder what it would be like to be buoyant all the time, a line of thought that led him to work with dolphins. Even as he searched for—and found—various ways to communicate with the large-brained sea mammals, however, Lilly maintained his newfound interest in mystical reality. In the early 1960s, he took LSD for the first time and began a new set of explorations.

Realizing that his scientific training gave him little background for interpreting his experiences, Lilly sought out philosophers, psychologists, and mystics to consult and compare notes. He worked on maps of uncharted levels of consciousness, correlating them with the states described by Gurdjieff and the Eastern mystics. Lilly also began to write popular books about the power of his discoveries, and he urged others to seek higher states of consciousness. In a 1972 book called *The Center of the Cyclone,* he asserted that if everyone on the planet regularly reached higher levels of awareness, problems such as pollution, famine, disease, and war would soon be solved through rational means. Lilly also affirmed that such consciousness raising could bring

immediate benefits on a smaller scale: "A corporation that encourages its management and its labor to achieve basic and higher levels of consciousness can show increasing efficiency, harmony, productivity, improved policies and better public relations within a few months. . . . The higher states of consciousness and the means of reaching them are an economic asset worth more money than one can currently measure."

The corporate world did not beat a path to Lilly's door, but he was not alone in his call to enhance institutional harmony—indeed to transform society itself—through concerted consciousness raising. Maharishi Mahesh Yogi, who preaches to a worldwide following from headquarters in Holland, teaches a form of mind expansion known as Transcendental Meditation—TM, for short. Like Lilly, the guru insists that the hope of a new world order lies in altered states of mind.

The guru's disciples point to an experiment in which some 11,000 inmates of prisons in Senegal were taught the TM program. Within a week, it is claimed, a dramatic improvement in the prison atmosphere was evident. Eventually, authorities reported a 70 to 80 percent drop in medical consultations and, most wondrous of all, an 85 percent drop in recidivism among released prisoners. On a grander scale, followers of the maharishi claim evidence to prove that when enough devotees practice TM in one place, the whole world's tensions and ills are reduced: Angry nations become less belligerent, sickness decreases, oil prices decline, and stock prices rise. On the strength of these claims, the maharishi has called for governments to fund a perpetual body of 7,000 TM disciples who, he insists, can create a "wave of coherence and harmony" that will decisively alleviate the world's afflictions and advance the goal of "bringing heaven on Earth for all mankind on a permanent basis."

The guru's grand scheme may never find a backer, but the idea of applying mind-altering techniques to achieve tangible benefits has held particular appeal for Americans, raised in a culture with a strong ethos of self-help. A typical

Maharishi Mahesh Yogi arrives in London from his native India in 1961, near the start of a ten-year mission to the West. The guru won popularity with his drug-free prescription for happiness and mind expansion through meditation. "Turning the attention inward," he taught, would put the conscious mind "in contact with the creative intelligence that gives rise to every thought."

early prophet of personal transformation was Napoleon Hill, author of the 1937 book *Think and Grow Rich.* The way to a life of harmony and prosperity, Hill believed, was through the subconscious mind. He taught a form of self-hypnosis called autosuggestion, by which a person could nourish the subconscious with "thoughts of a creative nature." Hill excited many followers with the promise that dramatic accomplishment awaited those who could envision themselves "on the road to success."

Those who carried Hill's self-help philosophy into the 1970s and 1980s were more sophisticated, tying their messages to lessons imported from Western science and Eastern religion. Best-selling American author Shakti Gawain propounded a technique called creative visualization: If a person could create a clear image of something desirable, then continue to focus on that image regularly, it would eventually become a reality. The goal might be physical—a new home or job, for example—or it might be improvement at an emotional, mental, or spiritual level. Creating and nurturing the internal experience, according to Gawain, will give rise to the external experience as well.

To explain the phenomenon, Gawain turned to modern physics. Matter, when viewed at atomic and subatomic levels, can be understood either as an aggregation of tiny particles or as a network of intertwined fields of energy. Because thought, too, is energy, Gawain avers, it can interact with the energy that makes up matter. Holding a clear idea firmly in the mind can "attract and create that form on the material plane," even without any direct action.

Along with such scientific-sounding descriptions of creative visualization, Gawain reinforces her position with assertions of a more mystical nature. She exhorts her readers, for example, to believe that "we are all in essence perfect, spiritual beings," and she suggests that by changing our innermost beliefs "we can eliminate illness and disease altogether." At a more practical level, Gawain and other proponents of creative visualization rely on techniques derived from the meditative practices of the East. Complete physical relaxation is the first step, combined with deep, slow, regular breathing. The visualization itself requires intense concentration on the desired image, in the way that a Buddhist monk, meditating on a holy phrase, repeats it over and over. Visualization techniques lend

The mind's powers to heal the body, overcome hardship, and reach new levels of awareness pervade the teachings of these four distinguished Americans. Mary Baker Eddy (top left) founded the Christian Science movement in 1876 after healing her own illnesses through Bible reading and prayer. Famed minister Norman Vincent Peale (top right), in his book entitled The Power of Positive Thinking, taught that with belief in oneself and in God, anyone can "conquer personal fear, triumph over adversity, and transform and enhance daily life."

Shakti Gawain (bottom left), whose Hindu first name means "energy," advocates "creative visualization" as a means of bringing goals into sharp focus and then realizing them. Journalist and educator Norman Cousins (bottom right) found that medical treatment is far more effective if bolstered by "hope, faith, love, will to live, purpose, laughter, and festivity." During his long and painful illness, to which he succumbed in 1991, Cousins said that "ten minutes of solid belly laughter would give me two hours of pain-free sleep."

themselves to many applications, from healthcare to sports. Some doctors teach patients to visualize their immune systems fighting off illness, thus empowering their natural defenses against disease. A cancer patient, for example, might imagine a tumor as a vicious animal surrounded by millions of white dogs—white blood cells—tearing it to pieces and devouring it. Some reports indicate that such visualizations may play a fundamental role in relieving symptoms and even in achieving cures.

Athletes frequently use visualization systems to achieve peak performance. Relaxed and removed from competitive pressure, an athlete imagines a specific action, such as a tennis stroke or a basketball shot, and repeats it over and over, mentally correcting for any errors. Studies show that mental "practice" for specific athletic skills can be as effective as physical drills, particularly if the visualizer can make real in his or her mind the sensory details of the drill—such as feeling a ball in the hands or hearing it bounce on the floor. Champion golfer Ben Hogan made it a habit to mentally rehearse each shot, trying to "feel" the club head meeting the ball and his club following through. Many other amateur and professional athletes, including Soviet Olympic competitors, make visualization a key element of their practice regimens.

One commercial mental-training program goes beyond simple visualization. In addition to supplying other teaching materials, it provides athletes with videotapes of an expert demonstrating skills over and over. The movement is shown at normal speed and in slow motion, and it is sometimes broken down into computerized graphics to illustrate the underlying mechanics. Music that accompanies the visuals accentuates the ideal tempo, rhythm, and timing of an optimal performance. After watching a tape, athletes are told to imagine performing each movement ten times in slow motion; regular repetition is said to promote the development of a "fluid and graceful rhythm" that parallels the skilled movement on the tape.

Visualization is only one of many learning techniques that seek to harness nonconscious levels of the mind. Research conducted in the early twentieth century indicated that people learned some things faster when training was supplemented with sleep learning. The instructional period for sailors learning Morse code, for instance, was reduced by three weeks when additional training was given during the sleeping hours. (Later research showed that the learning probably occurred when the trainees were not truly asleep but in a near-sleep state caused by the teaching itself.)

Newer learning systems take advantage of other states of consciousness that seem to share the heightened suggestibility of near sleep. Bulgarian psychiatrist Georgi Lozanov, after studying sleep learning and yoga, devised a technique that combines relaxation, repetition, and music to speed up learning of foreign languages. Music is a key ingredient. Lozanov's early research showed, not surprisingly, that when relaxed students tried to focus on learning, the stress of concentrating destroyed their relaxation. Then Lozanov found that when he played certain music—baroque orchestral pieces at a tempo of sixty beats per minute, to be exact—his subjects remained relaxed even while doing strenuous mental work. In some extraordinary all-day sessions under these conditions, his students were able to learn and retain more than 1,000 words of a foreign language, or nearly half of an everyday vocabulary.

All attempts at exploring and expanding the mind's potential notwithstanding, some theorists believe the next step for the human mind is to enter into a symbiosis with computers, actually moving human consciousness into more powerful, longer-lived machines. Subscribers to this idea cite the phenomenal development of computers in the last few decades, which has forced a reassessment of the meaning of the word *mind*. As the machines become faster and more capable, it gets harder and harder to tell if they are actually thinking, and a debate rages over whether machines can indeed become conscious.

In the most popular scenarios, the computers of today are merely ungainly precursors of wizard machines capable of a new kind of intelligence called post-biological, meaning that it does not spring directly from the human brain. This post-biological competence, also known as artificial intelligence, or AI, would eventually surpass human capabilities—all essential human functions would be matched by artificial counterparts. Machines would develop the ability to mastermind their own maintenance, reproduction, and improvement. The result would be intelligent robots, machines that would act and think like humans even if they bore little physical or mental resemblance.

The most sanguine AI champions foresee the emergence of a hybrid that combines the wisdom of the human mind with the power of the machine. Because the brain evolves so slowly, they say, humans' avid desire for greater knowledge and understanding can be met only by joining forces with computers. Some even imagine the most intimate union of these disparate minds—human and machine—in a phenomenon called transmigration. Since an ongoing computation can be halted in mid-process and transferred to a different computer, the argument goes, it follows that someday the memories and thought patterns within a human brain could be translated into computer language and moved over to a machine. One scenario has this transference happening piecemeal, with the human subject's brain being replaced section by section with computer units, until the flesh and blood organ is superseded altogether. Thus freed of its biological limitations, the human mind could experience in the material world the immortality it has always sought on the spiritual plane.

If the prospect of mechanical transcendence delights its advocates, it leaves others appalled. They see the specter of a future with computers in control, while the biological intelligence that created them dwindles in importance. Indeed, the computer era has given rise to numerous films, stories, and books that paint bleak pictures of machine-dominated futures. Before there can be any real understanding of future relations between humans and computers, however, a seemingly simple question must be

Aircraft Controlled by Thought Alone

Far from Hollywood, where screenwriters and special-effects experts have been staging such scenes for years, air force researchers are testing a highly advanced and imaginative set of aircraft controls. Unlike a steering stick, which requires touch to execute a maneuver, these new controls are operated by thought—or, more precisely, by brain waves, as represented in the composite photograph at right. So far, the system is earthbound, used only with a flight simulator in a laboratory at Wright-Patterson Air Force Base, near Dayton, Ohio. But some observers consider it a preview of the future.

The mind-driven controls are deceptively simple. Two fluorescent lights on the control panel flash on and off thirteen times a second, causing neurons in the pilot's visual cortex to fire at that frequency. Electrodes attached to the pilot's scalp relay his brain waves to a system that picks out the wave spiking thirteen times per second and measures it. The strength of that wave is displayed on the control panel. To maneuver the simulator, the flier consciously changes the strength of the brain wave. Suppressing it makes the simulator bank to the left; increasing the wave makes the simulator bank right; keeping the mind unengaged—but alert—holds the simulator level.

Not even Captain David Tumey, who heads the research project, can explain how people control their brain waves. "Some say that singing in your head raises the power," he offers, but other fliers just watch the bar scale as it registers change. They find the biofeedback-based system works remarkably well.

Tumey and his colleagues downplay the notion of pilots' one day roaring through dogfights on brain waves alone. For now, they want to know what stimulates brain waves, how they are related to thought, and how the waves differ from one person to the next. Nonetheless, the technology might help scientists determine how much information and how many tasks a pilot's brain can handle under stress—and how a computer might take on the overload.

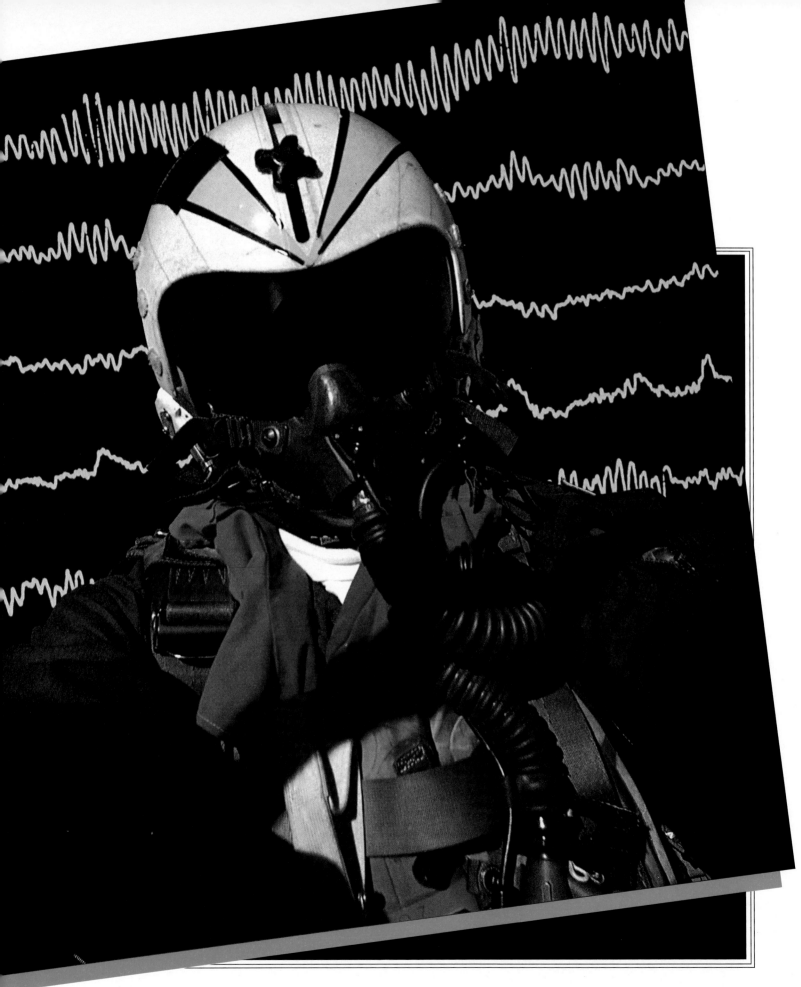

addressed: Can a machine duplicate the human mind?

The question, of course, brings to full circle the still unsolved problem of finding a satisfactory definition of mind. But one way to narrow the matter down is to ask if the computer can think. Alan Turing, a British mathematician who played a central role in the development of the first digital computers, was convinced that thought is essentially computational, and therefore something machines can do. In 1950, he proposed a classic test of the issue. Turing envisioned a human being in a room with a teletype machine. The person is not told whether the questions he or she sends via the teletype are being answered by another human or by a computer. If a computer is responding to the questions, said Turing, and if the person cannot tell whether the answers come from a human or from a computer, then it must be conceded that the computer can think.

One computer, created in the 1970s by AI researcher Kenneth Colby, succeeded in convincing a number of learned observers that it was human. The computer was programmed to imitate a person with paranoid tendencies and would sidestep questions it could not answer with agitated responses, such as "Maybe you have to watch out for the Mafia." After exchanging messages with the machine by teletype, several psychiatrists concluded that they were indeed conversing with someone whose powers of reasoning were somewhat impaired.

Even if they have not actually passed what is called the Turing test, some modern computers in a sense meet Turing's qualifications, at least in specialized tasks. A computer programmed to diagnose blood diseases, for example, can perform as well as any doctor. A chess-playing program can match skills with world-class players, while a backgammon program can beat them. Experts in AI predict that only time is needed to develop machines that will match the performance of human intelligence in every field. They make the analogy that if the sophisticated thinking machine of the future—the hardware—is compared to the brain, then the programs—software—that control the subtle interplay of electronic patterns correspond to the mind. Some people

actually suggest that if such a combination of hardware and software could do everything a human mind could do, then we would have to concede that it possessed consciousness and that it experienced thoughts, even feelings.

The idea of an artificial mind with thought, consciousness, and a variety of mental states runs counter to the common conviction that mental states are uniquely human attributes—not material, but spiritual. Many thinkers argue fiercely against the AI prognosis of mechanical consciousness. The brain-to-mind relationship, they say, is not equivalent to the rule-bound combination of computer and programs. The way thoughts emerge in the brain can never be described by a formal set of rules, or algorithms, of the sort needed to construct a computer program.

In fact, goes one powerful anti-AI argument, no computational process can ever explain subjectivity. If consciousness were simply a matter of computation, then a pocket calculator would be conscious. But a calculator can only compute; it cannot think about what it is working on or be subjective about what it is doing. To put it another way, the calculator only does what it is doing; the mind knows what it is doing. And since the human brain does not know how it knows what it knows—does not, that is, know the source of its own consciousness—there is no way it could build a machine that "knows."

Thus even the effort to build an artificial mind leads back to questions about the nature and source of human consciousness—the same questions pursued so long and ardently by philosophers and psychologists, mushroom eaters and mystics. And the answers to those questions are still being sought, both by explorers who deliberately venture outside the limits of the ordinary mind to probe the hidden domains that lie beyond and by orthodox exponents of scientific objectivity. Whether answers exist or not, the wonder of the quest for them is aptly captured in the words of explorer John Lilly: "The miracle is that the universe created a part of itself to study the rest of it, that this part, in studying itself, finds the rest of the universe in its own natural inner realities."

Strange New Universe

A surgeon in search of a tumor walks into a patient's brain, passing like magic through folds of gray matter. A tourist picnics on the moon. Enveloped in a steamy Mesozoic forest, awed schoolchildren watch a fierce tyrannosaur stalk his prey. However much these notions may read like science fiction, they are among very real possibilities opened up by a fast-growing technology called virtual reality.

"For humans to make their next leap in civilization," says Thomas Furness, an expert in the field, "I believe we have to combine the machine and human intellects." Virtual reality—also called "cyberspace" or "telepresence"—does exactly that. With sophisticated computer graphics, it creates astonishing artificial landscapes or translates real but inaccessible environments—the interior of a live human organ as revealed by a CAT scan, say—into worlds the user can enter and explore. By means of feedback systems and sensors that monitor body movements, the participant's mind is immersed in the machine-created realm and is voluntarily deceived into responding to it as if it were real.

"Virtual reality eliminates the separation between you and the computer," explains one virtual explorer. "You are within it." Some who speculate on the future of this strange new technology foresee a day when an air-traffic controller may reach out and touch a three-dimensional image of a moving aircraft to guide it to safety—or a time when people will be able to create and enter their own dream worlds.

Myron Krueger displays one of his more whimsical virtual-reality programs. Behind him, a small computer-generated figure dangles and jumps on the end of a virtual string, responding appropriately to movements of the enormously enlarged virtual arm and hand of the person demonstrating the program. "Pressing buttons, pushing levers, and turning knobs is not the stuff from which adventures are made," says Krueger. "One would prefer to step into the graphic world unencumbered and be able to move around freely within it."

Explorers of the Virtual Unknown

Myron Krueger was among the first to pioneer the idea of stepping into a computer-created world. In the 1970s he developed a system known as Videoplace, which projects a moving camera image of the participant onto a graphic scene. The impression of being absorbed into an artificial world is so convincing, Krueger reports, that people instinctively touch themselves to make certain they are still here.

Jaron Lanier, founder of Virtual Programming Languages, Inc., in California, discovered a different means of entering virtual reality. Lanier has developed "computer clothing," including an elaborate headpiece called an EyePhone. "The goggles put a small TV in front of each eye so you see moving images in three dimensions," he explains. "The goggles have a sensor to tell where your head is facing. What you see is created completely by the computer." A DataGlove, with sensors that register finger movements, completes the outfit. "If you hold your hand in front of your face, you see a computer-generated hand in the virtual world," says Lanier. "If you wiggle your fingers, you see its fingers wiggle." With the glove, a user can pick up a virtual ball and throw it.

"Sometimes I think we've uncovered a new planet," Lanier says, "one that we're inventing instead of discovering. We're just starting to sight the shore of one of its continents. Virtual reality is an adventure worth centuries."

Wearing his DataGlove and ready to don his EyePhone (at left in picture below), Jaron Lanier prepares to enter his virtual environment. Lanier, who believes that virtual technology is destined to become a powerful teaching tool, has illustrated its effectiveness by teaching himself how to juggle within his artificial world. "You learn to juggle in virtual reality by slowing down time and juggling with really slow balls," Lanier explains. "And then you gradually speed it up until it's the same speed as the real world."

Walk-In Blueprints and Brain Scans

Adventurous souls in various professions have already begun to put virtual reality to work. By translating blueprints into a visual structure, two architects tested the design of a proposed day-care center, moving through the rooms of a building that did not yet exist. Moreover, they virtually shrank themselves so they could view the center from a child's perspective. And a project at the San Diego Supercomputer Center enabled doctors to take a tour of a gigantic human brain. Physicians of the future may get a closeup look at problems by crawling around inside large virtual models of patients' bodies—created with input from modern scanning techniques such as computer axial tomography (CAT) and magnetic resonance imaging (MRI).

Using a computerized treadmill and a "magic helmet," an experimenter at the University of North Carolina (left) tours a building that has not been built. Through virtual reality, one architect discovered and corrected a design flaw before actual construction began.

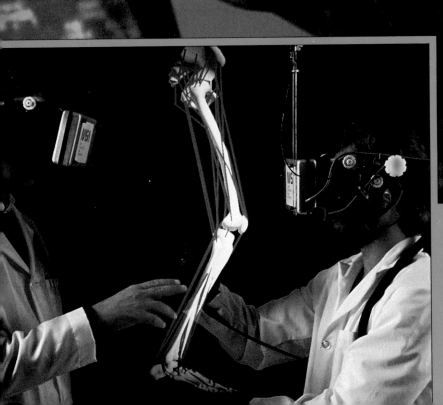

NASA scientists (near left) use goggles and sensor gloves hooked up to a computer to examine the leg of a virtual cadaver. With a virtual body and scalpel, says one researcher, "we could train surgeons in the same way that flight simulators are used to train pilots."

Demonstrating some futuristic technology, a University of Washington scientist wears a model of microlaser scanner glasses that one day are expected to project computer-generated images directly onto the user's retinas, thus delivering greater visual realism.

Pedaling through an imaginary countryside holds an added surprise for the virtual cyclist above—at a speed of twenty-five miles per hour, her bicycle will appear to leave the ground. "It was wonderful," enthused one rider of the flying bike. "I didn't want to take off the mask."

A video-arcade driving simulator with a "force feedback" steering wheel makes the ride so convincing that some drivers come prepared with motion-sickness medicine.

The Ultimate Video Game

Nearly any feat imaginable is possible in the virtual universe—swimming to the bottom of the ocean, riding a camel through the eye of a needle, leaping tall buildings at a single bound. With such adventures a mere computer chip away, many people see entertainment as the most obvious application for the new technology. Yet not all such uses are trivial amusements. With a tele-phone hookup, for example, an absent father could play catch with his children in a virtual ballpark. And virtual technology makes games and sports accessible to the physically disabled as never before. "Right now," says one scientist, "we can build virtual worlds for quadriplegics in which they can move and behave just as well as if they weren't handicapped."

Virtual sports enthusiast Chris Allis swings his racquet in anticipation of a racquetball game with a wheelchair-bound opponent. Although Allis runs, jumps, and dives for the ball as if playing a normal match, his opponent can easily keep up using simple hand movements.

In the cockpit of an F-111 fighter-jet simulator, an air force pilot "comes in for a landing" on a highly realistic, computer-generated airstrip. The image—richer in detail, sharpness, and color than the usual virtual-reality projection—is achieved through the use of a far more powerful computer than those employed in most systems.

An Infinity of Adventures to Come

"With the technology of virtual reality," declares Thomas Furness, director of Seattle's Human Interface Technology Laboratory, "we can change the world." Proponents of the phenomenon envision people going to work in virtual office buildings, traveling to virtual vacation resorts, and shopping at virtual malls—all without leaving home. The influence of virtual reality is expected to extend to other worlds as well. With data collected by unmanned NASA spacecraft, says research scientist Michael McGreevy, "we will be able to re-create the surface of Venus in virtual reality and explore it almost as you would your office."

Jaron Lanier views the technology's power in more personal terms. Babies, he says, have "an astonishing liquid infinity of imagination" that is thwarted by the resistance of the physical world—"a fundamental indignity." Virtual reality "doesn't resist us." It restores the infinite possibilities. "That's why virtual reality electrifies people," he says. "In the future I see it as a medium of communications where people improvise worlds instead of words, making up dreams to share."

ACKNOWLEDGMENTS

The editors wish to thank the following individuals and institutions for their valuable assistance in the preparation of this volume:
Patricia H. Allderidge, The Bethlem Royal Hospital Archives and Museum, Beckenham, Kent, England; François Avril, Conservateur, Département des Manuscrits, Bibliothèque Nationale, Paris; Joseph Carey, Society for Neuroscience, Washington, D.C.; Dr. Johann Feilacher, Haus der Künstler, Niederösterreichisches Landeskrankenhaus, Klosterneuberg, Austria; Dr. Thomas Furness, University of Washington, Seattle; David Goldblatt, Littleton, New Hampshire; Dr. John R. Hughes, University of Illinois Medical Center, Chicago; Bob Jacobson, University of Washington, Seattle; Professor Daniel Keyes, Ohio University, Athens; Myron Krueger, Vernon, Connecticut; Professor Luis Eduardo Luna, Swedish School of Economics, Helsinki, Finland; Dr. Peter Michel, Aquamarin Verlag, Grafing, Germany; Renato Minozzi, Centro di Telsen-Sao, Portogruaro, Rome; Laura del Pra, Centro di Telsen-Sao, Portogruaro, Rome; Dr. Richard Restak, Washington, D.C.; Dr. Johanna Senigl, Internationale Stiftung Mozarteum, Salzburg, Austria.

BIBLIOGRAPHY

Alexander, Franz G., *The History of Psychiatry.* New York: Harper & Row, 1966.

Bailey, Ronald H., *The Role of the Brain* (Human Behavior series). New York: Time-Life Books, 1975.

Barrett, William, *Death of the Soul: From Descartes to the Computer.* Garden City, N.Y.: Doubleday, 1986.

Benson, Herbert, and William Proctor, *Your Maximum Mind.* New York: Times Books, 1987.

Bermar, Amy, "Myron Krueger." *Network World,* February 4, 1991.

Blakemore, Colin, *Mechanics of the Mind.* Cambridge, England: Cambridge University Press, 1977.

Blakemore, Colin, and Susan Greenfield, eds., *Mindwaves: Thoughts on Intelligence, Identity and Consciousness.* New York: Basil Blackwell, 1987.

Blakeslee, Thomas R., *The Right Brain.* Garden City, N.Y.: Doubleday, 1980.

Bloom, Floyd E., and Arlyne Lazerson, *Brain, Mind, and Behavior.* New York: W. H. Freeman, 1988.

Borges, Jorge Luis. *The Aleph and Other Stories.* Transl. by Norman Thomas di Giovanni. New York: E. P. Dutton, 1970.

Bowers, Barbara, *What Color Is Your Aura?* New York: Pocket Books, 1989.

Brackman, Arnold C., *A Delicate Arrangement: The Strange Case of Charles Darwin and Alfred Russel Wallace.* New York: Times Books, 1980.

Brownlee, Shannon, "A Riddle Wrapped in a Mystery." *Discover,* October 1985.

Capra, Fritjof, *The Tao of Physics.* Toronto: Bantam Books, 1988.

Cardinal, Roger, *Outsider Art.* London: Studio Vista, 1972.

Castle, Kit, and Stefan Bechtel, *Katherine, It's Time: An Incredible Journey into the World of a Multiple Personality.* New York: Harper & Row, 1989.

Chance, Paul, "The Divided Self." *Psychology Today,* September 1986.

Chase, Truddi, *When Rabbit Howls: The Troops for Truddi Chase.* New York: Jove, 1990.

Cohen, Scott, *Creativity: What Is It?* New York: M. Evans, 1977.

Copony, Heita, *Mystery of Mandalas.* Wheaton, Ill.: Theosophical Publishing House, 1989.

Cousins, Norman:
Head First: The Biology of Hope. New York: E. P. Dutton, 1989.
"Proving the Power of Laughter." *Psychology Today,* October 1989.

Ditlea, Steve, "Grand Illusion." *New York,* August 6, 1990.

Druckman, Daniel, and John A. Swets, eds., *Enhancing Human Performance.* Washington, D.C.: National Academy Press, 1988.

Drury, Nevill, *The Elements of Human Potential.* Longmead, Dorset, England: Element Books, 1989.

Editors of Prevention Magazine Health Books, *Maximum Brainpower.* Emmaus, Penn.: Rodale Press, 1989.

Editors of Time-Life Books:
Cosmos (Voyage through the Universe series). Alexandria, Va.: Time-Life Books, 1989.
Mysteries of the Human Body (Library of Curious and Unusual Facts). Alexandria, Va.: Time-Life Books, 1990.
Psychic Voyages (Mysteries of the Unknown series). Alexandria, Va.: Time-Life Books, 1987.

Elvee, Richard Q., ed., *Mind in Nature.* San Francisco: Harper & Row, 1982.

Eros + Cosmos in Mandala (exhibition catalog). Tokyo: Seibu Museum of Art.

European Outsiders (exhibition catalog). Vienna, Austria: The Gérard A. Schreiner and John L. Notter Collection, 1986.

Evans, Hilary, *Alternate States of Consciousness: Unself, Otherself, and Superself.* Wellingborough, Northamptonshire, England: Aquarian Press, 1989.

Fackelmann, K. A., "Interviews Unmask Multiple Personalities." *Science News,* May 19, 1990.

Ferguson, Marilyn, *The Brain Revolution.* New York: Taplinger, 1973.

Friedman, Joe, "Freud's Guilty Secret." *The Unexplained* (London), Vol. 13, Issue 148.

Gaffney, Tim, "Tool Puts Mind over Matter." *Dayton Daily News,* June 24, 1990.

Gardner, R. Allen, Beatrix T. Gardner, and Thomas E. Van Cantfort, eds., *Teaching Sign Language to Chimpanzees.* Albany: State University of New York Press, 1990.

Gaunt, William, *Painters of Fantasy.* Oxford, England: Phaidon Press, 1985.

Gawain, Shakti, *Creative Visualization.* San Rafael, Calif.: New World Library, 1978.

Gawain, Shakti, and Laurel King, *Living in the Light.* San Rafael, Calif.: New World Library, 1986.

Gazzaniga, Michael S., "The Split Brain in Man." *Scientific American,* August 1967.

Gorney, Cynthia:
"One Woman Becomes 6 Witnesses at Rape Trial." *Washington Post,* November 8, 1990.
"Voices from a Fractured Past." *Washington Post,* November 10, 1990.

Goswamy, B. N., *Essence of Indian Art* (exhibition catalog). San Francisco: Asian Art Museum of San Francisco, 1986.

Graef, Hilda, *The Story of Mysticism.* Garden City, N.Y.: Doubleday, 1965.

Gregory, Richard, ed., *The Oxford Companion to the Mind.* Oxford: Oxford University Press, 1987.

Hamblin, Dora Jane, "Idiot Savants." *Life,* March 18, 1966.

Hayward, Jeremy W., *Perceiving Ordinary Magic: Science and Intuitive Wisdom.* Boston: New Science Library, 1984.

Herbert, W., "The Three Brains of Eve: EEG Data." *Science News,* May 29, 1982.

Hooper, Judith, and Dick Teresi, *The Three-Pound Universe.* New York: Dell, 1986.

Howe, Michael J. A., *Fragments of Genius: The Strange Feats of Idiots Savants.* London: Routledge, 1989.

Hughes, John R., et al., "Brain Mapping in a Case of Multiple Personality." *Clinical Electroencephalography,* Vol. 21, No. 4, 1990.

Huxley, Aldous, *Collected Essays.* New York: Harper & Brothers, 1923.

Into the Unknown. Pleasantville, N.Y.: Reader's Digest Association, 1981.

"Jaron Lanier." *Omni,* January 1991.

Jastrow, Robert, *The Enchanted Loom: Mind in the Universe.* New York: Simon and Schuster, 1981.

Jaynes, Julian, *The Origins of Consciousness in the Breakdown of the Bicameral Mind.* Boston: Houghton Mifflin, 1976.

Johnson, Robert, "Outer-Space Tunes Make Earth Debut in a Bar in Peoria." *The Wall Street Journal,* September 4, 1990.

Jung, Carl G., *Mandala Symbolism.* Transl. by R. F. C. Hull. Princeton, N.J.: Princeton University Press, 1972.

Jung, Carl G., et al., *Man and His Symbols.* Garden City, N.Y.: Doubleday, 1964.

Kenny, Michael G., *The Passion of Ansel Bourne.* Washington, D.C.: Smithsonian Institution Press, 1986.

Keyes, Daniel, *The Minds of Billy Milligan.* New York: Random House, 1981.

Kingston, Jeremy, *Healing without Medicine.* Garden City, N.Y.: Doubleday, 1976.

Klein, H. Arthur, *Graphic Worlds of Peter Bruegel the Elder.* New York: Dover, 1963.

Klingender, F. D., *Goya.* London: Sidgwick and Jackson, 1948.

Laing, R. D.:
The Politics of Experience. New York: Random House, 1967.
Wisdom, Madness and Folly: The Making of a Psychiatrist. New York: McGraw-Hill, 1985.

Leary, Timothy, *Flashbacks.* Los Angeles: J. P. Tarcher, 1983.

LeShan, Lawrence, *The Medium, the Mystic, and the Physicist: Toward a General Theory of the Paranormal.* New York: Viking Press, 1974.

Levy, Steven, "Brave New Worlds." *Rolling Stone,* June 14, 1990.

Lilly, John C., *The Center of the Cyclone: An Autobiography of Inner Space.* New York: Julian Press, 1985.

Ludtke, Melissa, "Can the Mind Help Cure Disease?" *Time,* March 12, 1990.

Luna, Luis Eduardo, "The Ayahuasca Visions of Pablo Amaringo." *Shaman's Drum,* summer 1990.

Luria, A. R., *The Mind of a Mnemonist.* Transl. by Lynn Solotaroff. Cambridge, Mass.: Harvard University Press, 1968.

MacGregor, John M., *The Discovery of the Art of the Insane.*

Princeton, N.J.: Princeton University Press, 1989.

Madigan, Carol Orsag, and Ann Elwood, *Brainstorms & Thunderbolts*. New York: Macmillan, 1983.

"Maharishi's Solution to International Conflicts Confirmed Again during Assembly." *MIU World* (Fairfield, Iowa), Vol. 1, No. 1.

Maranto, Gina, "The Mind within the Brain." *Discover*, May 1984.

Maxwell, Jessica, "Fantasia." *Omni*, June 1988.

"Mind over Matter." *Discover*, August 1990.

Mookerjee, Ajit, *Kundalini: The Arousal of the Inner Energy*. London: Thames and Hudson, 1989.

Moravec, Hans, *Mind Children: The Future of Robot and Human Intelligence*. Cambridge, Mass.: Harvard University Press, 1988.

Murray, David J., *A History of Western Psychology*. Englewood Cliffs, N.J.: Prentice-Hall, 1983.

Mysteries of the Unexplained. Pleasantville, N.Y.: Reader's Digest Association, 1982.

Navratil, Leo, "Art: Bridge between Normality and Psychosis." *DU*, September 1979.

"Norman Cousins Helps Other Patients As He Once Helped Himself—By Laughing." *Good Housekeeping*, November 1989.

Ostrander, Sheila, and Lynn Schroeder, with Nancy Ostrander, *Superlearning*. New York: Dell, 1979.

Ostrom, Joseph, *You and Your Aura*. Wellingborough, Northamptonshire, England: 1987.

Peale, Norman Vincent, *The Power of Positive Living*. New York: Doubleday, 1990.

Pearce, Joseph Chilton, *The Crack in the Cosmic Egg*. New York: Crown, 1988.

Pelletier, Kenneth R., *Toward a Science of Consciousness*. Berkeley, Calif.: Celestial Arts, 1978.

Penfield, Wilder:
The Mystery of the Mind. Princeton, N.J.: Princeton University Press, 1975.
No Man Alone: A Neurosurgeon's Life. Boston: Little, Brown, 1977.

Perrott, Roy, "The Man Who Says We're All Mad." *The Observer*, September 20, 1970.

Peterson, Ivars, "Combining a Person's Live Video Image with Computer Graphics Suggests Novel Ways of Working and Playing with Computers." *Science News*, June 22, 1985.

"Psychic Research: LSD—And All That." *Time*, March 29, 1963.

Rapoport, Judith, *The Boy Who Couldn't Stop Washing*. New York: E. P. Dutton, 1989.

"R. D. Laing." *Omni*, April 1988.

Ree, Jonathan, *Descartes*. New York: Pica Press, 1974.

Reed, Graham, *The Psychology of Anomalous Experience*. Buffalo: Prometheus Books, 1988.

Restak, Richard M.:
The Brain. Toronto: Bantam Books, 1984.
The Mind. Toronto: Bantam Books, 1988.

Rogo, D. Scott, *The Infinite Boundary*. New York: Dodd, Mead, 1987.

Roy, Archie:
"The Genius Within." *The Unexplained* (London), Vol. 11, Issue 126.
"Squatters in the Mind." *The Unexplained* (London), Vol. 10, Issue 119.

Sacks, Oliver, *The Man Who Mistook His Wife for a Hat*. New York: Harper & Row, 1987.

Sagan, Carl, *Broca's Brain*. New York: Random House, 1979.

Samuels, Mike, and Nancy Samuels, *Seeing with the Mind's Eye*. New York: Random House, 1975.

Schreiber, Flora Rheta, *Sybil*. Chicago: Henry Regnery, 1973.

Schul, Bill, *The Psychic Frontiers of Medicine*. New York: Fawcett, 1977.

Shelley, Mary, *Frankenstein, or, The Modern Prometheus*. Berkeley, Calif.: University of California Press, 1984.

Shepard, Leslie A., ed., *Encyclopedia of Occultism and Parapsychology*. Detroit: Gale Research, 1984.

Shone, Ronald, *Creative Visualization: How to Use Imagery and Imagination for Self-Improvement*. Rochester, Vt.: Destiny Books, 1988.

Sizemore, Chris Costner, *A Mind of My Own*. New York: William Morrow, 1989.

Smith, Anthony, *The Mind*. New York: Viking Press, 1984.

Sonneastro: Die Künstler aus Gugging (exhibition catalog). Vienna, Austria: Kulturabteilung und das Haus der Künstler in Gugging, 1990.

Stewart, Doug, "Through the Looking Glass into an Artificial World—Via Computer." *Smithsonian*, January 1991.

Stipp, David, "Does That Computer Have Something on Its Mind?" *The Wall Street Journal*, March 19, 1991.

Storr, Anthony, *Churchill's Black Dog, Kafka's Mice, and Other Phenomena of the Human Mind*. New York: Grove Press, 1988.

"Sun Myung Moon." *Time*, July 12, 1982.

Tansley, David V., *Subtle Body: Essence and Shadow*. New York: Thames and Hudson, 1988.

Taubes, Gary:
"Einstein's Dream." *Discover*, December 1983.
"Everything's Now Tied to Strings." *Discover*, November 1986.

Taylor, Eugene, *William James on Exceptional Mental States*. New York: Scribners, 1982.

Taylor, Gordon Rattray, *The Natural History of the Mind*. New York: E. P. Dutton, 1979.

Terrace, H. S., "How Nim Chimpsky Changed My Mind." *Psychology Today*, November 1979.

"This Is Tania." *Time*, June 3, 1974.

Treffert, Darold A., *Extraordinary People: Understanding Savant Syndrome*. New York: Ballantine Books, 1989.

"Voices from a Fractured Past." *Washington Post*, November 10, 1990.

Waldrop, M. Mitchell, *Man-Made Minds: The Promise of Artificial Intelligence*. Walker, 1987.

Wehr, Gerhard, *An Illustrated Biography of C. G. Jung*. Transl. by Michael H. Kohn. Boston: Shambhala, 1989.

Weil, Andrew, *The Natural Mind*. Boston: Houghton Mifflin, 1986.

"Why People Join." *Time*, December 4, 1978.

Wilbur, Ken, ed., *The Holographic Paradigm and Other Paradoxes*. Boston: New Science Library, 1985.

Wilson, Colin, *Mysteries*. New York: Pedigree Books, 1978.

Wing-Tsit Chan, *A Source Book in Chinese Philosophy*. Princeton, N.J.: Princeton University Press, 1963.

Yates, Frances A., *The Art of Memory*. Chicago: University of Chicago Press, 1966.

Yatri, *Unknown Man* (photographs). New York: Simon & Schuster, 1988.

Yeaple, Frank, "Live Video and Animated Graphics Are Interfaced Effortlessly." *Design News*, August 18, 1986.

Young, Patrick, *Schizophrenia*. New York: Chelsea House, 1988.

Yule, John-David, ed., *Concise Encyclopedia of the Sciences*. New York: Nostrand Reinhold, 1978.

Zukav, Gary, *The Dancing Wu Li Masters*. New York: William Morrow, 1979.

PICTURE CREDITS

Wolf/Visum, Hamburg; © Johann Feilacher, Haus der Künstler, Klosterneuburg, Austria (2). 66-69: © Johann Feilacher, Haus der Künstler, Klosterneuburg, Austria. 71: From *Das Mysterium des Mandalas* by Heita Copony, Aquamarin Verlag, Grafing, Germany, 1988. 72: Guttmann-Maclay Collection, Bethlem Hospital Museum, Beckenham, Kent. 73: Biblioteca Nacional, Madrid, from *Goya: In the Democratic Tradition* by F. D. Klingender, Sidgwick and Jackson, London, 1948. 74: Ann Ronan Picture Library, Taunton, Somerset. 75: Foto Claus Hansmann, Munich; Mary Evans Picture Library, London. 76: David Goldblatt, Littleton, New Hampshire—Camera Press, London. 77: David Goldblatt, Littleton, New Hampshire—Tony Buczko, Burch House. 80: Culver Pictures, Inc. 81: John R. Hughes, M.D., Ph.D., Department of Neurology, University of Illinois Medical Center at Chicago (2)—from *When Rabbit Howls* by Truddi Chase, Berkley/Jove, New York, 1990. 83: Courtesy Cornelia B. Wilbur, M.D., Lexington, Kentucky. 84, 85: Daniel Keyes—art by Billy Milligan, photographed by Daniel Keyes (6). 86: Courtesy Kit Castle; drawing by Kit Castle. 88: National Portrait Gallery, London—wood engraving by Barry Moser, from *Frankenstein* by Mary Shelley, © 1984 Pennyroyal Press. 89: Derek Bayes/Aspect Picture Library, London; Salzburger Museum Carolino Augusteum, Salzburg. 91: Giraudon, Paris. 93: Wade Davis (detail from page 95). 94, 95: The Bettmann Archive, New York; Wade Davis; Archiv für Kunst und Geschichte, Berlin. 96, 97: Herbert Benson, M.D., Harvard Medical School, New England Deaconess Hospital, Boston; Süddeutscher Verlag Bilderdienst, Munich (2). 98, 99: Archives Tallandier, Paris; The Bettmann Archive, New York; Kim Chon Kil/Gamma Liaison, New York (2)—Süddeutscher Verlag Bilderdienst, Munich. 101: From *Das Mysterium des Mandalas* by Heita Copony, Aquamarin Verlag, Grafing, Germany, 1988. 102, 103: The Bettmann Archive, New York. 105: Mary Evans Picture Library, London. 108, 109: Timothy Plowman—Pablo Amaringo, USKO-AYAR, Amazonian School of Painting, Pucallpa, Peru (2). 110, 111: Pablo Amaringo, USKO-AYAR, Amazonian School of Painting, Pucallpa, Peru. 112: Culver Pictures, Inc. 113: Wade Davis. 114, 115: From *Man and His Symbols* by Carl G. Jung et al., Doubleday, Garden City, New York, 1964; FPG, New York. 116: John Bryson. 118-121: Sergio Stingo, Naples. 123: FPG, New York. 124: Mary Evans Picture Library, London; Ron Galella Ltd., Yonkers, New York—New World Library, San Rafael, California; Steve Schapiro/Sygma, New York. 126, 127: Background photo Science Photo Library/Photo Researchers, Inc., New York—Joe Towers/Arms Communications, Woodbridge, Virginia. 129: © 1991 Peter Menzel, Napa, California (detail from page 133). 130-137: © Peter Menzel, Napa, California.

INDEX

TIME-LIFE BOOKS

EDITOR-IN-CHIEF: Thomas H. Flaherty

Director of Editorial Resources: Elise D. Ritter-Clough
Executive Art Director: Ellen Robling
Director of Photography and Research: John Conrad Weiser
Editorial Board: Dale M. Brown, Janet Cave, Roberta
Conlan, Robert Doyle, Laura Foreman, Jim Hicks, Rita
Thievon Mullin, Henry Woodhead
Assistant Director of Editorial Resources: Norma E. Shaw

PRESIDENT: John D. Hall

Vice President and Director of Marketing: Nancy K. Jones
Editorial Director: Russell B. Adams, Jr.
Director of Production Services: Robert N. Carr
Production Manager: Prudence G. Harris
Director of Technology: Eileen Bradley
Supervisor of Quality Control: James King

Editorial Operations
Production: Celia Beattie
Library: Louise D. Forstall
Computer Composition: Deborah G. Tait (Manager),
Monika D. Thayer, Janet Barnes Syring, Lillian Daniels
Interactive Media Specialist: Patti H. Cass

Time-Life Books is a division of Time Life Incorporated

PRESIDENT AND CEO: John M. Fahey, Jr.

Library of Congress Cataloging in Publication Data
The Mind and Beyond / by the editors of Time-Life Books.
p. cm.—(Mysteries of the unknown)
Includes bibliographical references and index.
ISBN 0-8094-6525-6
ISBN 0-8094-6526-4 (library)
1. Mind and body. 2. Dualism. 3. Brain. 4. Conscious-
ness. 5. Self.
I. Time-Life Books.   II. Series.
BF161.M54 1991
128'.2—dc20   91-81479
                                                        CIP

MYSTERIES OF THE UNKNOWN

SERIES EDITOR: Jim Hicks
Series Administrator: Jane A. Martin
Art Director: Tom Huestis
Picture Editor: Paula York-Soderlund

Editorial Staff for *The Mind and Beyond*
Text Editors: Janet Cave (principal), Robert A. Doyle
Senior Writer: Esther R. Ferington
Associate Editors/Research: Patti H. Cass, Christian D.
Kinney, Sharon Obermiller
Assistant Editor/Research: Denise Dersin
Assistant Art Director: Susan M. Gibas
Writers: Marfé Ferguson Delano, Sarah D. Ince
Senior Copy Coordinator: Colette Stockum
Copy Coordinator: Donna Carey
Picture Coordinator: Betty H. Weatherley
Editorial Assistant: Donna Fountain

Special Contributors: Jennifer Mendelsohn (lead research);
Ann Louise Gates, Sheila M. Green, Patricia A. Paterno,
Evelyn S. Prettyman, Nancy J. Seeger, Priscilla Tucker
(research); John Clausen, Margery A. duMond, Donald
Jackson, Alison Kahn, Harvey S. Loomis, Gina Maranto,
Susan Perry, Peter Pocock, Daniel Stashower (text); Sara
Schneidman (consultant); John Drummond (design); Hazel
Blumberg-McKee (index).

Correspondents: Elisabeth Kraemer-Singh (Bonn), Christine
Hinze (London), Christina Lieberman (New York), Maria
Vincenza Aloisi (Paris), Ann Natanson (Rome).
Valuable assistance was also provided by Li Yan (Beijing);
Otto Goblus, Robert Kroon (Geneva); Sian Stephenson
(Helsinki); Bing Wong (Hong Kong); Judy Aspinall (Lon-
don); Trini Bandrés (Madrid); Elizabeth Brown, Katheryn
White (New York); Dag Christensen (Oslo); Ann Wise,
Leonora Dodsworth (Rome); Mary Johnson (Stockholm);
Dick Berry, Mieko Ikeda (Tokyo); Traudl Lessing (Vienna).

Other Publications:

WEIGHT WATCHERS. SMART CHOICE
  RECIPE COLLECTION
TRUE CRIME
THE AMERICAN INDIANS
THE ART OF WOODWORKING
LOST CIVILIZATIONS
ECHOES OF GLORY
THE NEW FACE OF WAR
HOW THINGS WORK
WINGS OF WAR
CREATIVE EVERYDAY COOKING
COLLECTOR'S LIBRARY OF THE UNKNOWN
CLASSICS OF WORLD WAR II
TIME-LIFE LIBRARY OF CURIOUS AND UNUSUAL FACTS
AMERICAN COUNTRY
VOYAGE THROUGH THE UNIVERSE
THE THIRD REICH
THE TIME-LIFE GARDENER'S GUIDE
TIME FRAME
FIX IT YOURSELF
FITNESS, HEALTH & NUTRITION
SUCCESSFUL PARENTING
HEALTHY HOME COOKING
UNDERSTANDING COMPUTERS
LIBRARY OF NATIONS
THE ENCHANTED WORLD
THE KODAK LIBRARY OF CREATIVE PHOTOGRAPHY
GREAT MEALS IN MINUTES
THE CIVIL WAR
PLANET EARTH
COLLECTOR'S LIBRARY OF THE CIVIL WAR
THE EPIC OF FLIGHT
THE GOOD COOK
WORLD WAR II
HOME REPAIR AND IMPROVEMENT
THE OLD WEST

*For information on and a full description of any of the Time-
Life Books series listed above, please call 1-800-621-7026
or write:*
Reader Information
Time-Life Customer Service
P.O. Box C-32068
Richmond, Virginia 23261-2068

This volume is one of a series that examines the history
and nature of seemingly paranormal phenomena. Other
books in the series include: